VOGUE GUIDE TO
Crochet

STEIN AND DAY *Publishers* NEW YORK
IN ASSOCIATION WITH THE CONDÉ NAST PUBLICATIONS LTD

First published in the United States in 1972 . Reprinted 1974
by Stein and Day *Publishers*
in association with The Condé Nast Publications Ltd
Copyright © 1971 The Condé Nast Publications Ltd
Library of Congress Catalog Card No. 76-186218
All rights reserved
Printed in Great Britain . Collins Clear-Type Press
Stein and Day *Publishers* 7 East 48 Street, New York, N.Y. 10017
ISBN 0 8128 1433 9

Editor: Judy Brittain
Assistant Editor: Susan Read
Editor Condé Nast Books: Alex Kroll

Acknowledgements: Drawings: Barbara Firth. Photographers: Anthony Boase – page 49. Norman Eales – pages 37, 40, 56. Patrick Hunt – pages 38, 43, 45, 46, 50, 52, 54. Tessa Traeger – page 4. John Wingrove – pages 67, 68. Still life photography: Ronald Serbin and Maurice Dunphy. Malcolm Scoular – Front cover. John Wingrove – Back cover.

Abbreviations

alt	alternate
beg	begin(ing)
ch	chain
cl(s)	cluster(s)
cont	continue(ing)
dc	double crochet
dec	decrease
d tr	double treble
foll	following
h tr	half treble
inc	increase
no(s)	number(s)
oz(s)	ounces(s)
patt	pattern
rem	remaining
rep	repeat
sl st	slip stitch
sp	space
st(s)	stitch(es)
t ch	turning chain
tog	together
tr	treble
tr tr	triple treble

Contents

Introduction

Crochet is an exceedingly old and beautiful craft whose history is difficult to trace. It has been taken from one country to another, to a great extent by nuns, who have used and taught it for many generations. The word itself is French for 'hook'. Crochet has always been more popular abroad than in America, but during the nineteenth century it came into its own both for household and personal use. At this time its popularity grew in Ireland, where the thriving industry of crochet spread rapidly from homestead to homestead. Many very beautiful examples of crochet are in use today on church linen and vestments.

Now crochet has reached a new and very important fashion height and is seen in most boutiques and shops throughout Europe and the United States. To illustrate this fashion interest we have given a selection of designs ranging from a simple cardigan to a really beautiful fairytale wedding dress. All of which you will be able to make yourself.

The boom in crochet has also spread to household items such as bedspreads, cushions and even curtains. Once a bedspread has been made it will last for years and in time will become an object of pride and interest for children and grandchildren. We have given several patterns for bedspreads and also for cushions. With the cushion patterns it is simple to make more and more squares so that eventually you will have enough to join together and thus make a bedspread.

Crochet may also be used for trimming sheets, pillowcases, tablecloths, etc. and by adding a fringe or lace inset you will make a mundane article into something beautiful and unusual. We have given various ideas for these finishes at the end of the book.

Once the basic principles of crochet have been mastered it becomes quick and fascinating to work. It is important not to go too fast in the beginning stages but to read each page slowly and carefully before beginning to work the crochet. At first you may find that your work is tight and unsatisfactory, that your movements are awkward, but do not worry, just let the rhythm of yarn and hook take over. Soon you will find that the motion is becoming natural to you and then you will know you can crochet.

The look of crochet and fashion. Cushions designed by Tessa Traeger with instructions on page 69.

The ingredients

Crochet will undergo a complete change of mood depending on what size hook and weight of yarn is being used. For instance, a big hook and thick yarn will give a fabric warm and chunky enough for a blanket, whilst a very small hook and fine yarn will give an extremely delicate fabric suitable for the finest tablecloth or lacy trimmings. All the various ways and weights of crochet are illustrated in designs throughout the book.

Types of yarn

'Yarn' is the collective name for the threads which have been spun for crocheting. These threads can consist of wool, cotton, nylon, silk, hair, flax, hemp, metals or numerous man-made fibres, all of which can be used alone or in various combinations. These strands are known to the spinners as 'counts' and they, in turn, make up the ply, 2, 3, 4 or more, which make up the yarn. A ply can be any number of strands or counts and does not necessarily refer to the thickness of the yarn. It is for this reason that it is not advisable to substitute one yarn for another when working from a pattern. A 2-ply can be thicker than a 3-ply, as is the case with Shetland or other homespun yarns, and it is most important to use the particular yarn recommended for a design. The character of the yarn is determined in the process known as 'doubling', which forms a workable crochet yarn. If the twist of the yarn is tight, it will crochet up into a hard-wearing garment and is suitable for men's pullovers, socks and outer garments. Looser twisted yarns are more suitable for babies' wear, undergarments and bedjackets. In the case of man-made fibres used alone or in combination with wool, the yarn can be loose and yet very hard wearing. Fancy doubling or twisting produces bouclés, knop yarns and tweed wools. The character of any yarn is always taken into account when planning a design, and if the designer has stipulated a bouclé yarn, you will not obtain satisfactory results by using, say, a 4-ply crepe quality.

Types of hooks—see chart

Until recently, manufacturers of crochet hooks have made a separate range of wool and cotton hooks, but this has now been changed and all crochet hooks are supplied to an international standard so that the ranges of hooks, numbered from the largest size 7.00 to the smallest size 0.60, are now interchangeable.

It is essential to check any crochet instructions very carefully before commencing work to find the size and, if it is referred to, the range of hook used. The question of tension, partly governed by hook size, is of vital importance in order to obtain the correct measurements of anything you intend to make.

International standard sizes	Old U.K. sizes		American sizes	
	Wool	Cotton	Wool	Cotton
7.00	2	—	K	—
—	3	—	—	—
6.00	4	—	—	—
5.50	5	—	—	—
5.00	6	—	J	—
4.50	7	—	I	—
4.00	8	—	H	—
3.50	9	—	G	—
3.00	10	3/0	F	2/0
—	11	2/0	E	0
2.50	12	0	D	1
—	13	1	C	2
—	—	—	—	3
2.00	14	1½	B	4
—	—	2	A	5
1.75	15	2½	—	6
—	—	3	—	—
1.50	16	3½	—	7
—	—	4	—	8
1.25	—	4½	—	9
—	—	5	—	10
1.00	—	5½	—	11
—	—	6	—	12
0.75	—	6½	—	13
0.60	—	7	—	14
—	—	7½	—	—

How to begin

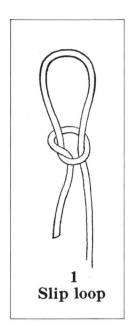

1
Slip loop

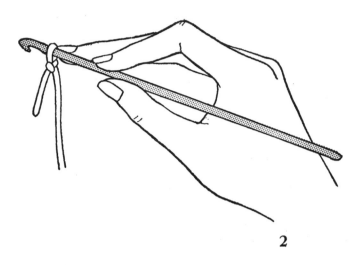

2

The majority of crochet begins with one single slip loop (fig. 1). Casting on in crochet is achieved by making the required length of chain loops, and the abbreviation for this is 'ch'. It is easier to learn to crochet by using a large hook and a double knitting yarn. The reason for this is that until you have learned to manipulate both the hook and the yarn you will find that you are inclined to work very tightly. Do not worry about your tension at this stage, but practise the first steps until you are completely relaxed. We will give a way of holding the hook and yarn as a guide, but the important thing is to develop a style which you find easy and comfortable. Do not become too discouraged with your first few efforts as a little practice and confidence will help you to achieve regular and even tension.

To work a chain
Put the slip loop first made on to the crochet hook, which should be held between the thumb and index finger of the right hand, having the middle finger resting close to the tip of the hook

and the shank held in the crook of the thumb and palm of the hand (fig. 2). If you find it more comfortable, hold the crochet hook between the thumb and middle finger of the right hand, with the index finger resting close to the tip of the hook and the shank held against the palm of the hand by the 3rd and 4th fingers (fig. 3). The yarn to be used should be held over the index and middle fingers of the left hand, under the 3rd finger and over the 4th finger, then a loop pulled from between the 3rd and 4th fingers and passed over the 4th finger (fig. 4). Holding the beginning of the slip loop between the index finger and thumb of the left hand, put the hook underneath the yarn in the left hand so that the yarn passes over the top of the hook and downwards on the side of the hook facing you (fig. 5). Draw the yarn through the slip loop, thus leaving the first loop below the new loop formed (fig. 6). Continue to lengthen the chain in this way by putting the yarn over the hook and drawing a new loop through the existing loop until the chain is the required length. When you have

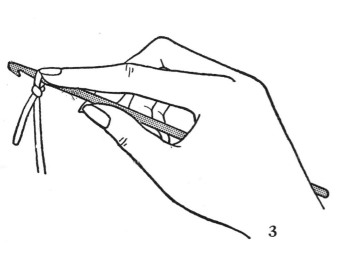

3

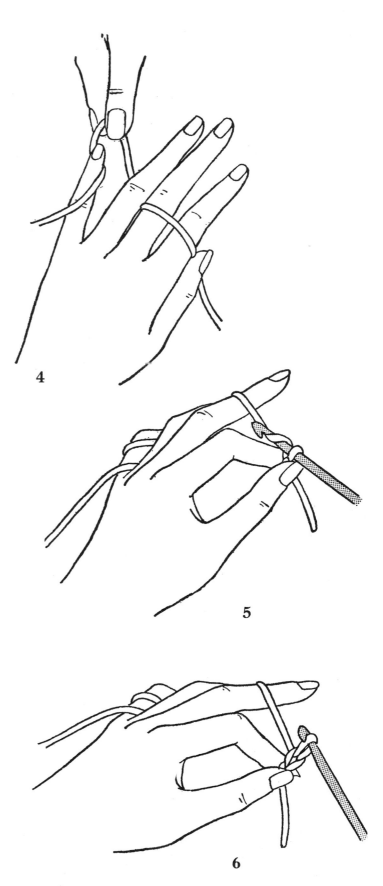

4

5

6

made the required number of chains you will have one loop left on hook which is *not* counted as a stitch. The abbreviation for this is 'ch'.

Turning chains

When working in rows in crochet, i.e. to and fro across the work and not in rounds, extra chains are added at the *end* of each row *before* turning the work to proceed with the next row. These chains form the first stitch of the next row, and the abbreviation for this is 't ch'. Where the number of stitches is given for any row for checking purposes, it will include the turning chain as the first stitch. The number of stitches required to form this turning chain depends on the stitch being used for the fabric, and the following table gives the usual number, unless otherwise stated in the pattern instructions:

Double crochet	–	1 turning chain
Half treble	–	2 turning chains
Treble	–	3 turning chains
Double treble	–	4 turning chains
Triple treble	–	5 turning chains

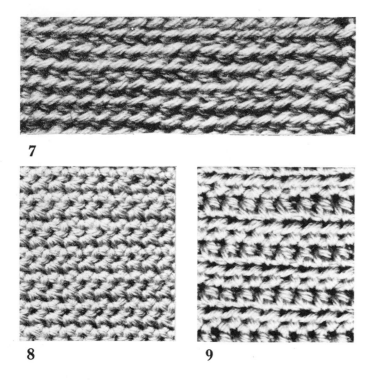

7

8

9

Basic stitches

10

11

12

All crochet patterns are based on the following stitches, either worked separately stitch by stitch to give an even fabric, or in combinations and groups to give various lace effects. Each of these stitches varies in length and twist, and where combinations are used to produce, say, a 'shell' pattern, the instructions will tell you how many of each type of stitch to work to give this effect. Practise these basic stitches in rows, holding your hook and yarn as given on page 8, until you can achieve a firm even fabric, paying particular attention to the paragraph on turning chains, see page 9.

Slip Stitch, sometimes called Single Crochet (fig. 7)

Work a chain of required length plus one turning chain, turn.

1st row: Miss the first chain from hook, ★ insert hook from front to back between 2 loops of next chain, yarn over hook, draw new loop of yarn through both chain and loop already on hook [1 slip stitch now formed and 1 loop on hook]; repeat from ★ to end of chain, make one turning chain to count as first stitch of next row, turn. Work following rows in the same way as 1st row, but miss the first slip stitch from hook and put the hook under the *double* loop at the top of each stitch on previous row and work last stitch into turning chain of last row. The abbreviation for this is 'sl st'. This is the shortest of all crochet stitches and is seldom used for a complete garment, although it is widely used in shaping and edgings and can be combined with other stitches to form a pattern.

Double Crochet (fig. 8)

Work a chain of required length plus one turning chain, turn.

1st row: Miss the first chain from hook, ★ insert hook from front to back between 2 loops of next chain, yarn over hook, draw new loop of yarn through chain [2 loops remain on hook], yarn over hook, draw new loop through both loops on hook [1 double crochet now formed and 1 loop on hook]; repeat from ★ to end of chain, make one turning chain to count as first stitch of next row, turn. Work following rows in same way as 1st row, but miss the first double crochet from hook and put the hook under the *double* loop at the top of each stitch on previous row and work the last stitch into the turning chain of the last row. The abbreviation for this is 'dc'.

Half Treble, sometimes called Short Treble (fig. 9)

Work a chain of required length plus 2 turning chains, turn.

1st row: Miss the first 2 chains from hook, ★ yarn over hook, insert hook from front to back between 2 loops of next chain, yarn over hook, draw new loop of yarn through chain only [3 loops remain on hook], yarn over hook, draw new loop through 3 remaining loops on hook [1 half treble now formed and 1 loop on hook]; repeat from ★ to end of chain, make 2 turning chains to count as first stitch on next row, turn. Work following rows in same way as 1st row, but miss the first half treble from hook and put the hook under the *double* loop at the top of each stitch on previous row and work the last stitch into the turning chain of the last row. The abbreviation for this is 'h tr'.

Treble (fig. 10)

Work a chain of required length plus 3 turning chains, turn.

1st row: Miss the first 3 chains from hook, ★ yarn over hook, insert hook from front to back between 2 loops of next chain, yarn over hook, draw new loop of yarn through chain only [3 loops remain on hook], yarn over hook, draw new loop of yarn through next 2 loops on hook [2 loops remain on hook], yarn over hook, draw new loop through 2 remaining loops on hook [1 treble now formed and 1 loop on hook]; repeat from ★ to end of chain, make 3 turning chains to count as first stitch of next row, turn. Work following rows in same way as 1st row, but miss the first treble from hook and put the hook under the *double* loop at the top of each stitch on previous row and work the last stitch into the turning chain of the last row. The abbreviation for this is 'tr'.

Double Treble, or Long Treble (fig. 11)

Work a chain of required length plus 4 turning chains, turn.

1st row: Miss the first 4 chains from hook, ★ yarn over hook *twice*, insert hook from front to back between 2 loops of next chain, yarn over hook, draw new loop of yarn through chain only [4 loops remain on hook], yarn over hook, draw new loop of yarn through next 2 loops on hook [3 loops remain on hook], yarn over hook, draw new loop of yarn through next 2 loops on hook [2 loops remain on hook], yarn over hook, draw new loop of yarn through 2 remaining loops on hook [1 double treble now formed and 1 loop on hook]; repeat from ★ to end of chain, make 4 turning chains to count as first stitch of next row, turn. Work following rows in same way as 1st row, but miss the first double treble from hook and put the hook under the *double* loop at the top of each stitch on previous row and work the last stitch into the turning chain of the last row. The abbreviation for this is 'd tr'.

Triple Treble (fig. 12)

Work a chain of required length plus 5 turning chains, turn.

1st row: Miss the first 5 chains from hook, ★ yarn over hook 3 *times*, insert hook from front to back between 2 loops of next chain, yarn over hook, draw new loop of yarn through chain only [5 loops remain on hook], yarn over hook, draw new loop of yarn through next 2 loops on hook [4 loops remain on hook], yarn over hook, draw new loop of yarn through next 2 loops on hook [3 loops remain on hook], yarn over hook, draw new loop of yarn through next 2 loops on hook [2 loops remain on hook], yarn over hook, draw new loop of yarn through 2 remaining loops on hook [1 triple treble now formed and 1 loop on hook]; repeat from ★ to end of chain, make 5 turning chains to count as first stitch of next row, turn. Work following rows in same way as 1st row, but miss first triple treble from hook and put the hook under the *double* loop at the top of each stitch on previous row and work the last stitch into the turning chain of the last row. The abbreviation for this is 'tr tr'.

Tension

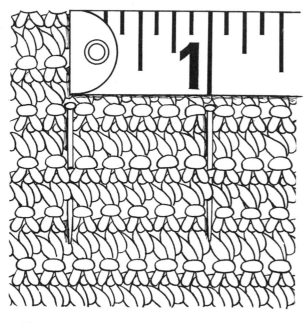

13

All reliable crochet patterns will state the number of stitches and, where possible, the number of rows to a given measurement – usually one inch – and also the correct number and type of hook and yarn which the designer has used to produce the garment. Because crochet is an exceedingly 'personal' craft resulting in enormous variances between one worker and another, it is of the *utmost* importance that you obtain the same number of stitches to the given measurement, but it does not matter in the least if you have to use several sizes smaller or larger hook to achieve this measurement. Confusion has been caused in the past by some books stating that a certain size of hook is 'correct' for a certain thickness of yarn, which has led many readers to use the size stated without first checking their own tension, in the belief that the exact results would thus be obtained. It must be remembered that when a particular tension is stated in a pattern it means that this tension has been worked by a designer, and unless you work to the same tension you will not achieve the same results. Using the correct yarn and crochet hook stated, if the tension is given as, say, 4 trebles to the inch, and your tension is $4\frac{1}{2}$ trebles to the inch, your fabric will be too tight, and if your tension is $3\frac{1}{2}$ trebles to the inch your fabric will be too loose. Even a quarter of a stitch difference can make an overall difference in measurements of 2 inches or more.

How to check your tension

Before commencing any garment, work a small sample about 4 inches square in the main pattern and on the hook stated. Place the sample on a flat surface and mark out one inch with pins (fig. 13). Count the number of stitches and rows very carefully, and if your tension is correct then you can begin the design of your choice. If you have any doubt at all, mark out 2 or even 3 inches with pins as a further check. If you have

**The vital point
of achieving
correct tension in crochet
is possibly the most
important factor
in successful work and,
as in knitting,
the one step so often
overlooked**

fewer stitches to the inch than stated your tension is too loose and you should work another sample using a size smaller hook. If you have *more* stitches to the inch then your tension is too tight and you should work another sample using a size larger hook. Continue in this way, altering the size of your hook until you obtain the correct tension given – only then is it safe to start the pattern.

Often when people begin to crochet, because they are tense, they will in fact be working too tightly, and will get too many stitches to the row, as in Sample 2. After some practice, the rhythm of hook and yarn will soon be felt, and the fabric will become looser and easier to work. However, should your natural tension still be on the tight side for the tension required in the pattern, then change to a larger hook (Sample 1). Conversely, once the rhythm of hook and yarn has been felt, your tension may be very loose, and once more the hook size will need to be changed, this time to one size smaller.

These two rather exaggerated samples will give you some idea of the difference in tension when a pattern is made up by two workers who have very different natural tensions, and from them you will begin to see that the question of tension cannot be stressed too often or too strongly. Perhaps tension will be easier to understand when one realises that crochet has been chosen to make a fabric, whether it be plain, lacy, closely worked, or patterned. You will note that, in the instructions given for many of the crochet garments included in this book, alternative hook sizes in both the old and new ranges have been given, where applicable. A few minutes spent in checking this vital point will avoid disappointment with the finished garment.

Do NOT read beyond this chapter until you have mastered all the preceding stages.

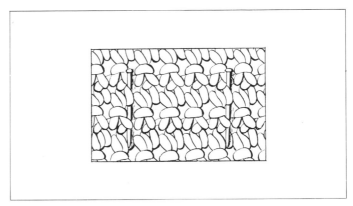

Sample 1

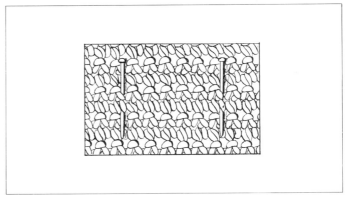

Sample 2

Shaping

14

All shaping is worked by adding to or taking away from the number of stitches on a row. Increasing a stitch means adding a stitch, and decreasing a stitch means losing it. It must be borne in mind that the average row in crochet is much deeper than in knitting, so when shaping a garment care must be taken not to decrease or increase in such a way as to leave an uneven edge, which could cause difficulty in making up the garment. Most reliable patterns give shaping in detail, but you will find that many give instructions for decreasing by omitting the first and last stitches on a row, and increasing by working twice into the first and last stitches on a row. This, however, is liable to produce a very uneven edge which will prove awkward and untidy to seam when the garment is ready to be made up. The following methods of shaping are very neat and give a most satisfactory finish.

Decreasing

To cast off in crochet
Work the required number of rows, *omitting* the turning chain at the end of the last row. On the next row work in slip stitch over the number of stitches to be cast off, now work the turning chain to count as the first stitch of this row, miss the first stitch from hook then work in pattern to the end of the row. If groups of stitches are to be cast off at each end of the row, work as given above, then work in pattern to the required number of stitches from the end of the row, work the turning chain and turn. If stitches are to be cast off on the *following* row, omit the turning chain at the end of the row (fig. 14).

To decrease a stitch
Unless a pattern is being used where individual decreasing instructions are given, work the turning chain to count as the first stitch in the usual

15

way, miss the 2nd stitch from hook, work in pattern to the last 2 stitches, miss the next stitch and work the last stitch, then work the turning chain. If a long stitch, such as double or triple treble is being worked, an alternative method of decreasing avoids a gap which tends to form where the missed stitch would have been. In this method the turning chain forms the first stitch, then work the 2nd stitch in the usual way, *omitting* the last stage [2 loops remain on hook], work 3rd stitch also omitting the last stage [3 loops remain on hook], yarn over hook, draw new loop of yarn through all loops on hook, leaving one loop on hook. In this way, the 2nd and 3rd stitches become one stitch only at the top of the stitch, thus giving the correct number of stitches for the following row, but filling what would otherwise be a space at the base of the stitches. The same method can be used at the end of a row, taking the 2nd and 3rd from last stitches together and working the last stitch in the usual way (fig. 15).

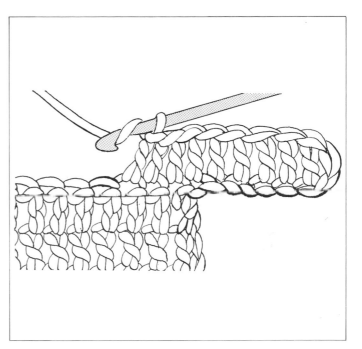

16

Increasing

To cast on in crochet
Work the required number of rows, *omitting* the turning chain at the end of the last row. Work a chain for the required number of stitches to be cast on plus the turning chain, turn. Count the turning chain as the first stitch, then work in pattern across other chain stitches and to end of row (fig. 16).

To increase a stitch
Work the turning chain to count as the first stitch, then work 2 stitches into the 2nd stitch and 2 stitches into the 2nd from last stitch, work last stitch in the usual way, work the turning chain to count as first stitch of the next row (fig. 17).

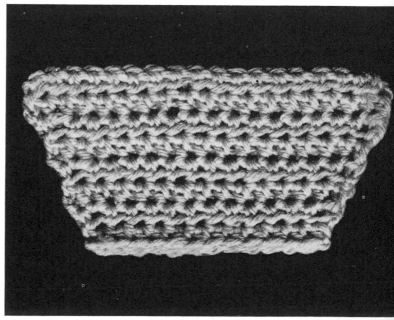

17

Crochet stitches

Ridged treble (fig. 18)
With this stitch both sides of the work are alike. Work as given for Treble, see page 11, but work into the back loop *only* of the loop at the top of each stitch.

Ridged treble (fig. 19)
With this stitch the right side of the work only is ridged.
1st row: Work as given for Treble, see page 11.
2nd row: Work as given for Treble, working into the back loop *only* of the loop at the top of each stitch.
3rd row: Work as given for Treble, working into the front loop *only* of the loop at the top of each stitch. Repeat the 2nd and 3rd rows throughout to form pattern.

You will find it helpful to work some of these stitch samples as it will accustom you to the rhythm and terminology of crochet

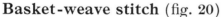

Basket-weave stitch (fig. 20)

This is a variation of treble stitch, formed by putting the hook round the stem of the treble from the back or the front, NOT using the loops at the top of the stitches.

Work a chain having multiples of 6 plus 2 turning chain.

1st row: 1 treble into 3rd chain from hook, 1 treble into each chain to end, 2 chain, turn.

2nd row: Yarn over hook, insert hook from back of work between 1st and 2nd stitches round 2nd stitch and back between 2nd and 3rd stitches, draw new loop of yarn through and work 1 treble in usual way, work 2 more trebles in this way on next 2 stitches – called 3 tr Bk – * yarn over hook, insert hook from front of work between next 2 stitches round stitch and back between next 2 stitches, draw new loop of yarn through and work 1 treble in usual way, work 2 more trebles in this way on next 2 stitches – called 3 tr Ft – work 3 tr Bk; repeat from * to last 3 stitches, work 3 tr Ft on next 3 stitches, 2 chain, turn.

3rd and 4th row: As 2nd.

5th row: * Work 3 tr Ft, 3 tr Bk; repeat from * to end, 2 chain, turn.

6th and 7th row: As 5th.

Repeat the 2nd to 7th rows throughout to form pattern.

Crazy pattern (fig. 21)

Work a chain having multiples of 4 plus 8 chain.

1st row: Miss 3 chain, work 3 treble into next chain, miss 3 chain, work 1 double crochet into next chain, * work 3 chain, work 3 treble into *same* chain as double crochet was worked, miss 3 chain, work 1 double crochet into next chain; repeat from * to end of row, 3 chain, turn.

2nd row: Work 3 treble into double crochet of previous row, * 1 double crochet into top of 3 chain loop on previous row, work 3 chain, work 3 treble into same chain loop as double crochet was worked; repeat from * to end of row, ending with 1 double crochet into last loop, 3 chain, turn.

Repeat the 2nd row throughout to form pattern.

Crochet stitches

Shell pattern (fig. 22)

Work a chain having multiples of 8.

1st row: Miss 3 chain, work 5 treble into next chain, miss 3 chain, ★ work 1 double crochet into next chain, miss 3 chain, work 5 treble into next chain, miss 3 chain; repeat from ★ ending with 1 double crochet, 3 chain, turn.

2nd row: Work 3 treble into double crochet of previous row, ★ work 1 double crochet into 3rd treble of 5 treble shell of previous row, work 5 treble into the next double crochet of previous row; repeat from ★ ending with 3 treble to form half a shell, 3 chain, turn.

3rd row: Work 5 treble into double crochet between half shell and first complete shell on previous row, ★ work 1 double crochet into 3rd treble of next 5 treble shell of previous row, work 5 treble into next double crochet of previous row; repeat from ★ to end of row, ending with a complete shell and 1 double crochet, 3 chain, turn.

Repeat the 2nd and 3rd rows throughout to form pattern.

Bobble stitch (fig. 23)

Work required length of chain, turn.

1st row: Work 1 double crochet into 3rd chain from hook, 1 double crochet into each chain to end, 3 chain, turn.

2nd row: ★ Yarn round hook, insert hook into next stitch, draw 1 loop through loosely, [yarn round hook, insert hook into same space, draw loop through loosely] twice, [7 loops on hook], yarn round hook and draw through 7 loops, 1 double crochet into next stitch; repeat from ★ to end, 2 chain, turn.

3rd row: Work 1 double crochet into back loop of each stitch to end, 3 chain, turn.

Repeat the 2nd and 3rd rows throughout to form pattern.

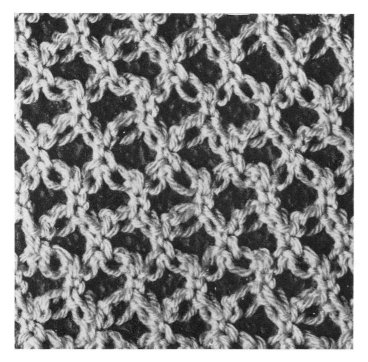

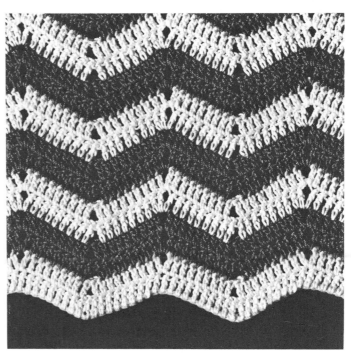

King Solomon's knot (fig. 24)

1st row: Put a slip loop on hook and make 1 chain through slip loop, ★ draw loop up to ½", yarn over hook, draw new loop of yarn through forming a loose chain stitch, insert hook between double and single loop of chain stitch and draw yarn through, yarn over hook, draw new loop of yarn through both loops on hook making one knot stitch; repeat from ★ to required length, make one more knot stitch with ¾" loop and one with ⅜" loop, turn.

2nd row: Work 1 double crochet into 3rd knot stitch from hook, ★ work 2 knot stitches drawing loop out to ⅜", work 1 double crochet into next knot stitch of previous row; repeat from ★ working 1 double crochet at end of row into first chain of commencing row, make 1 knot stitch with ¾" loop and 1 knot stitch with ⅜" loop, turn.

3rd row: Work 1 double crochet into 4th knot from hook, work as given for 2nd row working last double crochet into knot in centre of turning stitches.

Repeat the 3rd row throughout to form pattern. To work the last row work 1 knot stitch with ½" loop between double crochet to correspond with 1st row.

Note: When the loop is drawn out to the required length, it should be held firmly in the left hand between thumb and fingers to prevent it slipping until the knot is completed.

Chevrons (fig. 25)

Note: Mc = main colour; cc = contrast colour.

Using Mc, commence with a length of ch having a multiple of 19 ch plus 4.

1st row: 1 tr into 4th ch from hook, 1 tr into each ch, 3 ch, turn.

2nd row: Miss first 2 tr, ★ 1 tr into each of next 8 tr, into next tr work 1 tr 2 ch and 1 tr [a V st made], 1 tr into each of next 8 tr, miss 2 tr; rep from ★ ending with miss 1 tr, leaving the last loop on hook work 1 tr into next ch, drop Mc, pick up cc and draw through rem 2 loops, 3 ch, turn. [Always change colours in this way.]

3rd row: Miss first 2 tr, ★ 1 tr into each of next 8 tr, a V st into sp of next V st, 1 tr into each of next 8 tr, miss 2 tr; rep from ★ ending with miss 1 tr, 1 tr into next ch, 3 ch, turn.

4th row: As 3rd, dropping cc and picking up Mc, 3 ch, turn.

5th row: As 3rd.

6th row: As 3rd, dropping Mc and picking up cc, 3 ch turn. Rep 3rd to 6th rows for length required, omitting t ch at end of last row. Fasten off.

Crochet stitches

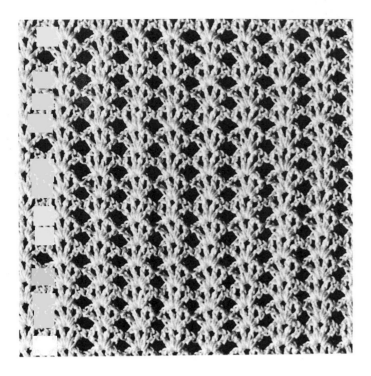

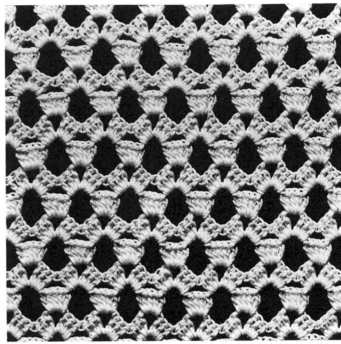

Stitch in blocks (fig. 26)

Commence with a length of ch having a multiple of 4 ch plus 3.

1st row: Into 7th ch from hook work [1 tr, 1 ch] 3 times and 1 tr [a shell made], ★ miss 3 ch, into next ch work [1 tr, 1 ch] 3 times and 1 tr [another shell made]; rep from ★ to within last 4 ch, miss 3 ch, 1 tr into next ch, 3 ch, turn.

2nd row: A shell into centre sp of first shell, ★ a shell into centre sp of next shell; rep from ★ to within last shell, a shell into centre sp of next shell, miss next sp of same shell, 1 tr into next ch, 3 ch, turn.

Rep 2nd row for length required, omitting t ch at end of last row. Fasten off.

Lace shell pattern (fig. 27)

Commence with a length of ch having a multiple of 6 ch plus 3.

1st row: 4 tr into 6th ch from hook, ★ 4 ch, miss 5 ch, 5 tr into next ch; rep from ★ to within last 9 ch, 4 ch, miss 5 ch, 4 tr into next ch, miss 2 ch, 1 tr into next ch, 3 ch, turn.

2nd row: 2 tr into first tr, ★ into next sp work 3 tr 3 ch and 3 tr; rep from ★ ending with miss 4 tr, 3 tr into next ch, 6 ch, turn.

3rd row: ★ 5 tr into next 3 ch sp, 4 ch; rep from ★ to within last sp, 5 tr into next ch sp, 3 ch, 1 tr in 3rd of 3 ch, 6 ch, turn.

4th row: 3 tr into first sp, ★ into next sp work 3 tr 3 ch and 3 tr; rep from ★ to within last sp, 3 tr into next sp, 3 ch, 1 tr into 3rd of 6 ch, 3 ch, turn.

5th row: 4 tr into first 3 ch sp, ★ 4 ch, 5 tr into next sp; rep from ★ to within last sp, 4 ch, 4 tr into next sp, 1 tr into 3rd of 6 ch, 3 ch, turn.

Rep 2nd to 5th rows for length required, omitting t ch at end of last row. Fasten off.

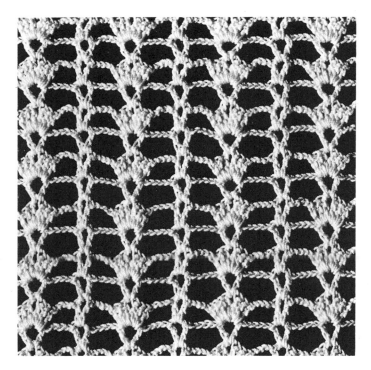

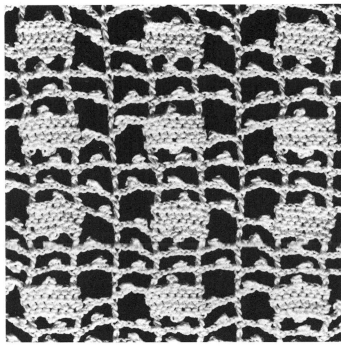

Shell and trellis pattern (fig. 28)

Commence with a length of ch having a multiple of 12 ch plus 7.

1st row: Into 5th ch from hook work 1 tr 2 ch and 1 tr [a V st made], * 4 ch, miss 5 ch, into next ch work 1 tr 2 ch and 1 tr [another V st made]; rep from * to within last 2 ch, miss 1 ch, 1 tr into next ch, 3 ch, turn.

2nd row: A V st into sp of first V st, * 4 ch, into sp of next V st work 3 tr 2 ch and 3 tr [a shell made] 4 ch, a V st into sp of next V st; rep from * ending with 1 tr into next ch, 3 ch, turn.

3rd row: A V st into sp of first V st, * 4 ch, a V st into sp of next shell, 4 ch, a V st into sp of next V st; rep from * ending with 1 tr into 3rd of 3 ch, 3 ch, turn. Rep 2nd and 3rd rows for length required, omitting t ch at end of last row. Fasten off.

Trellis pattern (fig. 29)

Commence with a length of ch having a multiple of 15 ch plus 8.

1st row: 1 dc into 3rd ch from hook [a picot made], 2 ch, 1 tr into 10th ch from picot, * 5 ch, a picot, 2 ch, miss 4 ch, 1 tr into next ch; rep from * ending with 8 ch, turn.

2nd row: A picot, 2 ch, miss first tr, * 1 tr into next tr, 5 ch, a picot, 2 ch; rep from * ending with miss 2 ch after next picot, 1 tr into next ch, 8 ch, turn.

3rd row: A picot, 2 ch, miss first tr, 1 tr into next tr, * 5 ch, a picot, 2 ch, 1 tr into next tr, 1 ch, turn, 1 dc into each of next 7 sts working behind picot, 1 ch, turn, [1 dc into each dc, 1 ch, turn] twice, 1 dc into each of next 4 dc, 3 ch, 1 dc into last dc, 1 dc into each of next 3 dc [a block made], 5 ch, a picot, 2 ch, 1 tr into next tr, 5 ch, a picot, 2 ch, 1 tr into next tr; rep from * omitting 5 ch, a picot, 2 ch and 1 tr at end of last rep and working last tr into 3rd of 8 ch, 8 ch, turn.

4th row: * A picot, 2 ch, 1 tr into next dc, 5 ch, a picot, 2 ch, miss next 2 dc, a picot and 2 dc, 1 tr into next dc, 5 ch, a picot, 2 ch, 1 tr into next tr, 5 ch; rep from * omitting 5 ch at end of last rep and working last tr into 3rd of 8 ch, 8 ch, turn.

Rep 2nd to 4th row for length required, omitting t ch at end of last row. Fasten off.

Working from a pattern

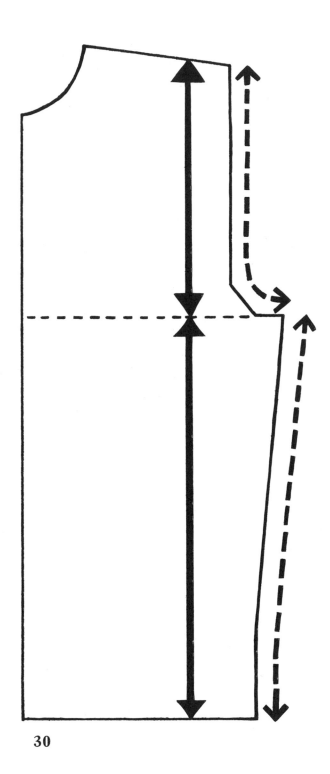

Choosing your pattern

Before beginning any crochet design it is advisable to make sure that you are not being too ambitious at first – it is much better to complete a simple cushion cover or baby's blanket rather than starting on a complicated dress pattern which may have you floundering after the first few rows and will eventually remain unfinished. Always read right through a pattern before starting to crochet to make sure it is not too difficult, particularly the making-up section, as a plain but tailored coat will entail as much in making up as in all the work which has gone before.

In this book the following patterns are simple to work and good ones to start on: the matinee jacket, the baby's shawl, the front cover shawl, and both the cushion designs.

Materials

Once you have chosen your design, it is absolutely essential to buy sufficient yarn to complete the article. Only by using this one yarn throughout can you be sure that you will obtain an even tension and that your garment will work out to the measurements given. It is extremely unwise to try and substitute a different yarn, especially now-a-days when there are so many types on the market; different yarns of the same ply will all vary slightly. If you are in any doubt about which yarn to use, write to your nearest spinner with details of the hook size specified for the article, the tension to be worked and the weight of wool suggested, e.g. 4-ply; the spinner should be able to suggest a yarn which can be worked within those specifications.

Do remember to buy extra yarn if you wish to add to the measurements given in the pattern. Keep a ball band from one ball of yarn, which

30

will quote the exact shade and dye lot number, in case you do need extra.

Measurements

Nearly all patterns give instructions for more than one size, with the first set of figures referring to the smallest size and figures for larger sizes in brackets, thus, 32″ (34″–36″) bust. Based on these sizes, if you are making a garment in a 36″ bust, the number of stitches and measurements for your size will be shown as the second set of figures in brackets throughout, unless only one set of figures is given, which will apply to all sizes. Before beginning your pattern you may find it easier to go through and mark the figures given for your size. Measurements for body and sleeve lengths will be given in the pattern and if you want to add to any of these always remember to allow for extra yarn.

Your work should be placed on a flat surface and measurements taken from the *centre* of the work and not at the edges (fig. 30). Adjustments can be made to the length of the body by adding or taking away rows *before* the armhole shaping is reached. Where there is side shaping on the body or sleeves, adjust the length when the shaping has been completed. Be very accurate about measuring armhole depth – never on the side curve and never try to alter the length here if possible as the correct fit of the sleeves depends on the correct armhole depth. Remember to work the same number of rows on pieces which have to be joined, for example, the front and back of a garment – a row counter can be useful here.

Tension

Do not miss this paragraph – it is vital to the success of your work. See page 12.

31

Joining in a new ball

Always join in a new ball of yarn at the beginning of a row if possible. If the yarn has to be joined in the middle of the work, which is necessary when working in rounds, the ends should be spliced. Unravel the ends of yarn of the ball being used and the new ball, cut away one or two strands from each end, overlay the two ends and twist together until they hold. The twisted ends should be of the same thickness as the original yarn. Work very carefully with the newly twisted yarn for a few stitches, then trim away the odd ends of yarn. If you cannot join in the yarn at the beginning of a row *never* crochet a knot into your work but splice the ends as described (fig. 31).

Working from a pattern

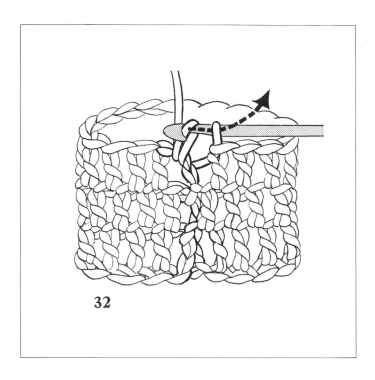

32

shaping, however, the beginnings and ends of the pattern rows will change. With patterns made up from basic stitches this is no problem, as you can see how to work each stitch from what has gone before. With more elaborate patterns you should analyse how the stitch works, then work in your extra stitches accordingly. With complicated lace stitches it may be best to work the increased stitches in double crochet or trebles depending on the basic stitch of the pattern until there are sufficient extra stitches to work another complete pattern. Keep a check on rows with a row counter so that you know exactly which pattern row you are working and when the next piece of shaping is due.

Abbreviations

See 'Abbreviations', page 3. The abbreviations for any unusual or difficult stitches will be given in individual instructions.

Methods of working

Working to and fro in rows

Commencing with a chain of the required length, the work is turned at the end of each row, see 'Turning chains', page 9. Work continues in this way, row by row, until required length is achieved.

Working in rounds

Commencing with a given chain, this chain is formed into a circle by joining the last chain

Mistakes

If these occur there is only one solution and that is to unpick work back to the error and correct it.

Patterned stitches

The number of stitches cast on for each piece are calculated to fit the pattern exactly, so that for the first few rows you can follow the instructions without any alteration and get to know the pattern sequence. As soon as you start any worked to the first chain by means of a slip stitch. Further rounds are then worked into this circle, each round being completed by means of a slip stitch into the first stitch of the round, or as stated in the instructions (fig. 32).

Working motifs

Some designs are based upon a number of small units or motifs, and very attractive results can be obtained by combining different shapes. Details of the motif used and the making up will be given in the instructions, and in some cases, once the first motif is completed, the second motif is joined to this as part of the pattern on the last round. Where this is not given, the correct number of motifs must be worked, and these are then sewn or crocheted together (fig. 33).

Joining in new colours for motifs

Instructions for splicing are given on page 23. Splicing is the most professional method for joining in a new colour or new ball of yarn, however a further method is as follows: Fasten off old colour or yarn then put hook back into same place and with new colour put yarn over hook and pull it through so that you have a loop on hook. Work one chain with double yarn using both the short end and the working end then proceed with pattern. When work is complete sew in all ends.

Both these methods are used for working in rows or rounds.

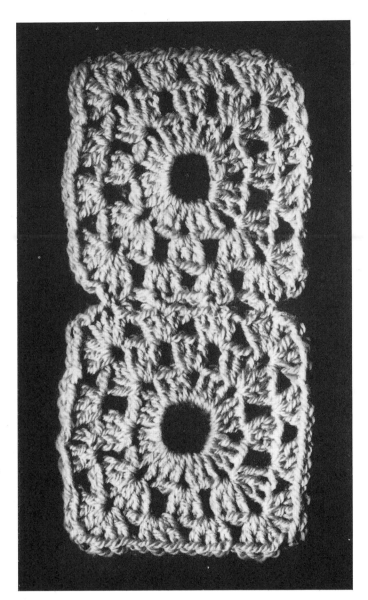

33

Finishing touches

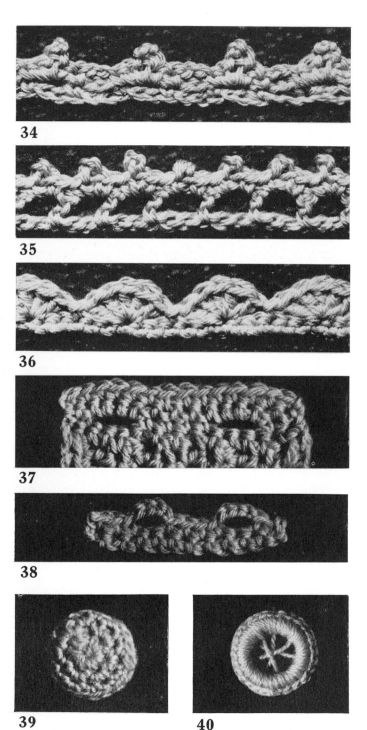

34

35

36

37

38

39   **40**

Because of the depth of crochet stitches and the thickness of the fabric it is not generally desirable to have a turned under hem, and most reliable patterns will give instructions for neatening hems and edges, either by means of rows of double crochet or with special stitch effects. We give below instructions for three edgings which can be used to give an attractive finish, some buttoning ideas, and fine picots for delicate crochet.

Edgings

Small picot edging (fig. 34)
Make a chain of multiples of 6 plus 2, turn.
1st row: 1 dc into 2nd ch from hook, * 2 ch, miss 2 ch, 1 dc into next ch; rep from * to end, 1 ch, turn.
2nd row: * 1 dc into space, 3 ch, 1 sl st into first of these 3 ch to form picot, 1 dc into same space, 1 dc into next dc, 2 ch, miss 2 ch, 1 dc into next dc; rep from * to end.

Picot edging (fig. 35)
Make a chain of multiples of 3 plus 5, turn.
1st row: Work 1 tr into 8th ch from hook, * 2 ch, miss 2 ch, 1 tr into next ch; rep from * to end, 3 ch, turn.
2nd row: * 1 dc into first 2 ch space, 3 ch, 1 dc into first of these 3 ch to form picot, 1 dc into same space; rep from * into each space to end.

Scallop edging (fig. 36)
Make a chain of multiples of 6, turn.
1st row: * Miss 2 ch, work 5 tr into next ch, miss 2 ch, 1 sl st into next ch; rep from * to end.

Buttonholes

Chain buttonhole
Work one row of dc along edge of work where buttonholes are required. On the 2nd row of dc, buttonholes are made by missing the number of stitches required for the width of the button and working a chain of the same number. On the

3rd row work dc into the space left by the chain, making sure that there are the same number of dc as there are ch. Work a final row of double crochet. The number of rows and position and size of the buttonholes depend on the garment design (fig. 37).

Loop buttonhole
Work one row of dc along edge of work where buttonholes are required. On the 2nd row of dc a loop of ch is made of sufficient size to slip over the button. This loop may be strengthened by being covered by a close row of dc worked into and around loop (fig. 38).

Covered buttons
Crochet covered buttons are a simple way of obtaining perfectly matching buttons. They may be round button moulds covered in crochet or a ring covered with crochet.

Round buttons (fig. 39)
Work 3 ch and join into a circle with a sl st.
1st round: Work 6 dc into circle, joining with a sl st into first dc.
2nd round: Work 2 dc into each dc of previous round, joining with a sl st into first dc.
3rd round: Work 1 dc into each dc of previous round, joining with a sl st into first dc. Repeat 3rd round until button mould is covered.
Last round: * Miss 1 dc, 1 dc into next dc; rep from * to end, joining with a sl st into first dc.
Slip crochet cover over button mould and draw together under button, leaving an end of yarn for sewing on button. An additional trim may be added by working one row of sl st around outer edge of button after cover has been made.

Ring buttons (fig. 40)
Work a round of close dc all round ring, joining with a sl st into first dc. Across back of ring work strands of yarn diagonally across ring and sew to garment through centre of these threads.

41

42

43

Fine picots

Top (fig. 41)
MATERIALS: J. & P. Coats 6/C Crochet Cotton No. 20. New International size No. 1.25 crochet hook.
TENSION: Width of trimming ⅛".
* 4 ch, 1 dc into 4th ch from hook; rep from * for length required. Fasten off.

Centre (fig. 42)
MATERIALS: J. & P. Coats 6/C Crochet Cotton No. 20. New International size No. 1.25 crochet hook.
TENSION: Width of trimming ¼".
* 5 ch, 3 tr into 4th ch from hook; rep from * for length required. Fasten off.

Bottom (fig. 43)
MATERIALS: J. & P. Coats 6/C Crochet Cotton No. 20. New International size No. 1.25 crochet hook.
TENSION: Width of trimming ⅜".
4 ch, * 3 d tr into 4th ch from hook, 1 sl st into same ch, 6 ch; rep from * for length required. Fasten off.

Making up

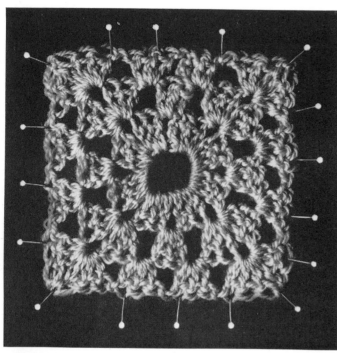

44

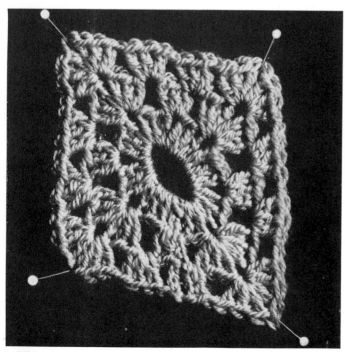

45

Pressing

Before making up instructions are given, most patterns will give pressing details, but the following points will prove very useful:

Wool
Press under a damp cloth with a warm iron.

Mixtures of wool and any man-made fibres
Press *lightly* under a damp cloth with a warm iron.

Nylon
Press under a *dry* cloth with a warm iron.

Mohair
Press *lightly* under a damp cloth with a warm iron.

Courtelle (100% Acrylic yarn)
Do not press.

Acrilan
Do not press.

Cotton
Press under a damp cloth with a fairly hot iron.

Embossed patterns
These should be *steamed* rather than pressed, using a very damp cloth and holding the iron over the surface, simply to make steam and not using any pressure. This will even up and neaten the work without flattening or spoiling the pattern.

Angora
Steam as given for embossed patterns.

When pressing is directed pin out pieces on to a flat surface using plenty of pins and taking care to keep stitches and rows in even lines (fig. 44). It is essential not to pull the work out of shape by pinning too tightly or unevenly (fig. 45). Place each piece right side down on to a well-padded surface, taking care to keep the stitches and rows running in straight lines. Press the main part of each piece as given in the instructions. Wait until the fabric has cooled then take out the pins.

Seams

Use a blunt-ended wool needle and the original yarn for sewing together. If the yarn is not suitable for sewing use a 3-ply yarn in the same shade. On an even patterned garment such as double crochet, half treble or treble crochet seams may be joined by a single row of double crochet, great care being taken to ensure that the seam is the same length as the finished garment and that you have not stretched it or pulled it too tightly (fig. 46). Woven flat seams and backstitch seams may be used where they prove suitable. More open patterns obviously require the use of a woven flat seam to bring the two edges together without any ridge forming.

46

Woven flat seam
With the right sides of the work facing each other, place your finger between the two pieces to be joined, insert the needle from the front through both pieces below the corresponding pips, pull the yarn through and insert the needle from the back through both pieces the length of a small running stitch, pull the yarn through. Repeat this along the seam matching the 'pips' on each piece. The seam will then be drawn together and will be flat and very neat when pressed. This method is always used for baby garments, ribbing and underclothes (fig. 47).

Backstitch seam
This method is firm, yet elastic, keeps the garment in shape and will not break if roughly treated. Place the two pieces to be joined right sides together, join in the sewing yarn by making 3 small running stitches over each other one stitch in from the edge. Put the needle back into

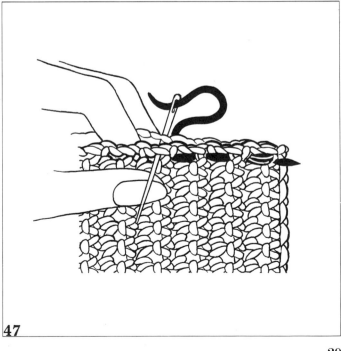

47

Making up

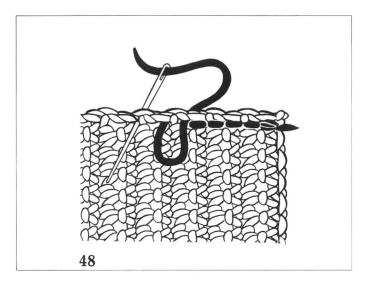

48

the beginning of the running stitch and pull the yarn through, insert the needle from the back through the fabric and beyond the first running stitch the length of another small stitch and pull the yarn through. Repeat this along the seam, keeping stitches neat and even and one stitch in from the edge of both pieces of fabric and taking great care not to split the knitted stitches (fig. 48). Your pattern will tell you which seams to sew first, but they are usually worked in the following order:

Shoulder seams
Backstitch firmly one stitch from the edge, taking the stitching across the steps of shaping in a straight line. Press on the wrong side. For heavy sweaters, reinforce these seams with ribbon or tape.

Set in sleeves
Mark centre top of sleeve and pin in position to shoulder seam, then pin cast off stitches to cast off underarm stitches of body. Keeping the sleeve smooth on either side of the shoulder seam, work fine backstitch round the curves as near the edge as possible.

Side and sleeve seams
Join with backstitch in one complete seam as near the edge as possible.

Sewing on collars
Place right side of collar to wrong side of neck, matching centre backs and taking care not to stretch the neckline. Join with a firm backstitch as near the edge as possible.

Sewn-on bands
Sewn-on bands worked separately. Use a woven flat seam matching row for row.

Sewn-on pockets or any applied band or decoration
Use slip stitching, taking care to keep the line

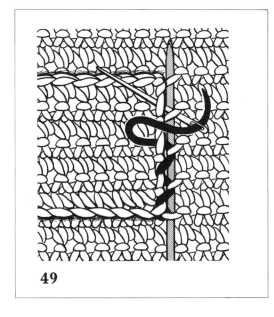

49

absolutely straight. A good way to ensure a straight sewing line is to thread a fine knitting needle, pointed at both ends, under every alternate stitch of the line you wish to follow and catch one stitch from the edge of the piece to be applied and one stitch from the needle alternately, using matching yarn (fig. 49).

Skirt waist

Skirt waist using casing or herringbone stitch. Cut elastic to the size required and join into a circle. Mark off the waistline of the skirt and the elastic into quarters and pin elastic into position on the wrong side, taking care to distribute the work evenly. Hold the work over the fingers of the left hand and with the elastic slightly stretched work a herringbone stitch, catching the elastic above and below as you work (fig. 50).

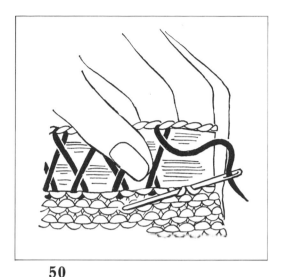

50

Ribbon facing

Lightly press the part to be faced before sewing on the ribbon, taking care not to stretch the edge. Choose a soft ribbon, available in a wide selection of colours and widths from most stores. When facing buttonhole bands, the ribbon should be wide enough to cover the strip with $\frac{1}{4}''$ to $\frac{1}{2}''$ to spare on either side and a $\frac{1}{2}''$ hem top and bottom. Take great care not to stretch the crochet when measuring the ribbon lengths, and cut the facing for buttonhole and button bands at the same time, so that they match exactly. Fold in the turnings, pin ribbon to the wrong side, easing the crochet evenly and checking that the buttonholes are evenly spaced. With matching silk, slip stitch with the smallest possible stitches along all edges. Cut buttonholes along the straight grain of the ribbon, remembering to make them wide enough for the buttons. Oversew the ribbon and crochet together to avoid fraying, then neaten by working buttonhole stitch round the buttonhole with the original yarn (fig. 51).

Grosgrain ribbon can be shaped to fit a curved

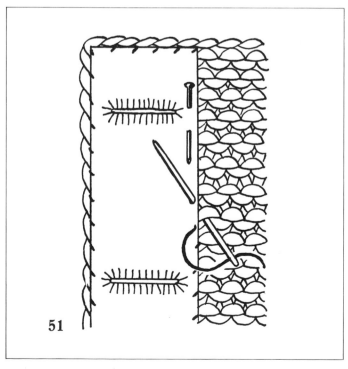

51

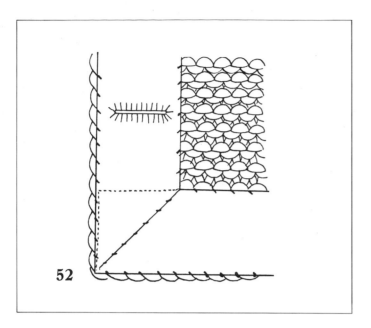

52

Making up

edge by pressing with a hot iron and gently stretching one edge until the desired curve is made.

When facing with ribbon on two edges at right angles, seam outside edge in place first, then fold ribbon into a mitred corner before seaming inside edge (fig. 52).

Decorative seam
Lapped seams can be used on yokes and square-set sleeves when a firm fabric stitch has been worked. Place the parts to be joined right sides together, with the underneath part projecting $\frac{1}{2}''$ beyond the upper part. Backstitch along edge, turn to the right side and backstitch $\frac{1}{2}''$ from the first seam through both thicknesses of fabric, taking care to keep the line of stitching straight and even.

Shrinking
Provided 100% pure wool has been used, parts of garments which have been stretched can be shrunk back into place. Place the part to be shrunk face down on to a well-padded surface, pat and pin into shape and size required. Cover with a wet cloth and hold a hot iron over the cloth to make plenty of steam. Alternatively steam then pat into shape, taking out the pins as soon as possible, until the required shape is achieved, then leave without handling until quite dry.

Sewing in zip fasteners
Pin in the zip to the opening, taking great care not to stretch the crochet. Sew in zip using backstitch, keeping the grain of the crochet straight. Except on very heavy garments, it is better to use Nylon zips because of their lightness and flexibility (fig. 53).

Skirt lining
It is generally accepted that it is better not to

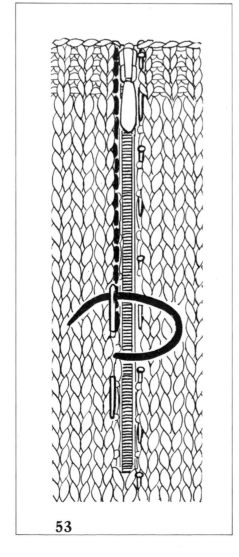

53

line a crochet skirt but to wear a waist-length slip. If you cannot purchase this ready-made, buy lining material the exact shade of your skirt, press the crochet pieces and cut lining pieces to match the skirt, allowing extra width for waist, seams and hems. Pin in waist darts in lining to fit crochet, stitch darts, sew seams and lower hem, turn in the seam allowance at top and oversew to waist of skirt. Finish with a petersham waistband, hooks and eyes, and sew in zip fastener. Do not sew the lining to seams or hem of the crochet skirt.

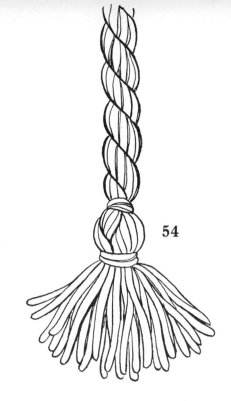

54

Twisted cords

The number of strands of yarn used to make a twisted cord depends on the thickness required. For a baby garment in 3 or 4-ply, 4 strands of yarn are used. Two people are required for this, and the length of each strand should be three times as long as the required cord. Each person takes one end of the strands, stand facing each other and holding the yarn taut. Twist the strands towards the *right* until a firm twist has been obtained along the whole length of the strands. Still holding the strands taut, fold the cord in half lengthwise, knot together the two loose ends and the cord will form when it is smoothed downwards from the knot between the fingers. Trim with a tassel or pom-pom (fig. 54).

Tassels

Length and thickness of tassels can be varied as required. Cut a piece of cardboard 2″ wide, wind yarn several times round cardboard and cut through yarn at one edge of cardboard only. Thread the pieces of yarn through the cord in half, finishing by winding the yarn several times round the top folded ends about $\frac{1}{2}$″ down from the end of the cord. Sew in loose end of yarn and trim loose ends of tassel (fig. 55).

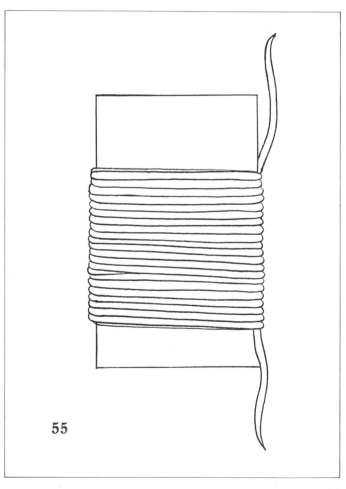

55

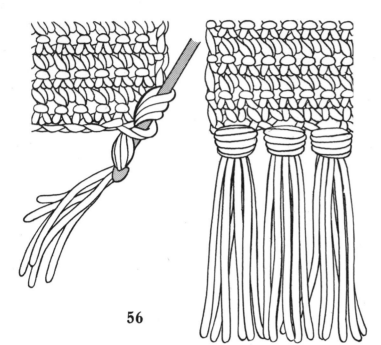

56

Fringing

Unless precise length is given in the instructions, cut strands of yarn approximately 8″ long and place in groups of 3 or 4 strands according to the thickness required. With the wrong side of the edge to be fringed facing you, insert a crochet hook as near the edge as possible, fold strands in half to form a loop, put loop on hook, pull through edge of work, place hook behind all strands of yarn and draw through loop. Continue along edge in this way at regular intervals until completed. Trim ends of fringing to neaten (fig. 56).

Pom-poms

Cut two circles of cardboard the size you require the finished pom-pom to be and cut out a circular hole in the centre of each – the larger the hole the thicker the pom-pom. Wind the yarn evenly round the two pieces of cardboard and through the centre hole until the hole is filled, and you have to put the last strand through with a threaded needle. Break off the yarn. Cut through the yarn at the outer edge of the cardboard only, firmly tie a piece of yarn round the cut pieces between the two circles of cardboard, and when strands are secured cut away the cardboard and leave end of yarn for sewing on. Shake well and trim ends into shape (fig. 57).

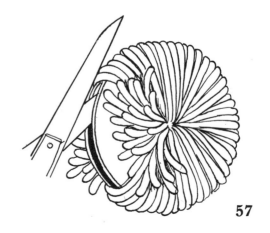

57

If you are left-handed

If you are left-handed and would like to learn to crochet, all the same basic principles will apply. The right-handed worker holds the hook in her right hand and controls the yarn with her left hand, working across the work from the right-hand edge to the left-hand corner. For the left-handed worker, the reverse of this will apply.

The hook is held in the left hand between the thumb and first finger, with the middle finger resting lightly against the tip of the hook and the shank held in the crook of the hand between the thumb and palm. The yarn is held and controlled by the right hand, exactly as given for the left hand, and the row is begun at the left-hand corner and worked across until the right-hand edge is reached.

If the illustrations given in this book confuse you, a mirror may be placed in front of the illustration to reflect it. This will then give the correct position for the left-handed worker.

Hints on care and washing

Pure wool
Although many hand-knitting wools are now given shrink-resist finishes, the structure of hand-knitted fabrics makes elementary care in washing essential if the best results are to be obtained. If hand-knitted garments are never allowed to become badly soiled they will be easily washable, and it is important to remember that pure wool stays clean longest.

Washing should be done in warm, *not* hot, water. Detergents and soap powders should always be dissolved completely and never brought into direct contact with the garments. Rubbing should be avoided and the lather gently squeezed through the fibres. All traces of soap or detergent should be rinsed out in tepid water. A loose wringer or a spin dryer may be used to remove surplus water. Wringing by hand should be avoided. The garment should then be arranged on a clean smooth surface and gently eased into its original shape. If it is finally dried on a clothes horse the sleeves should not be allowed to hang down. When dry the garment should be lightly pressed on the wrong side with a warm iron over a damp cloth.

Courtelle (100% Acrylic yarn)
Warm wash (40°C) as soon as the garment gets soiled. Use soapless detergent or, if your water is soft, soap flakes or powder dissolved in water pleasantly hot to the hand. Rinse thoroughly. Remove excess moisture by squeezing lightly, or rolling in a towel, or give a short spin dry. Finally, smooth garment and dry flat away from direct heat. Courtelle garments can be machine-washed, following instructions for delicate fabrics. When garment is completely dry, fold neatly and store in a drawer, not on a hanger.

Nylon
Wash often – wash soon. All Nylon garments can be washed by hand or by machine. Use hot water (60°C, 140°F) for 'whites', and hand-hot (48°C, 118°F) for 'coloureds'. Use a synthetic detergent in hard water districts and dissolve thoroughly. Rinse until the water is clear. Do not wring knitwear but squeeze and dry flat. If spin drying is required, stop after the first rush of water from the outlet ceases.

If absolutely necessary synthetics may be pressed with a cool iron and a dry cloth.

Evening suit

Instructions are for a 34″ bust. Changes for 36″ and 38″ sizes are given in brackets.

MATERIALS: Jacket. 15(16–17) ozs standard 3-ply yarn. **Skirt.** 17(18–20) ozs of same yarn. Crochet hook, New International size No. 3.50 (size G). Waist length of elastic.

MEASUREMENTS: Jacket. To fit a 34″ (36″–38″) bust. Length to shoulder: 21″(21″–21½″), adjustable. Sleeve seam: 18″, adjustable. **Skirt.** To fit 36″(38″–40″) hips. Length: 24″(24″–25″), adjustable.

NOTE: For extra length add 1 oz of yarn per 1″.

TENSION: 6½ sts and 3 rows to 1″ over patt.

SKIRT

FRONT: Beg at waist. With No. 3.50 hook make 106 (112–118) ch. **Base row:** Work 2 tr 1 ch 2 tr into 3rd ch from hook – called 1 shell –* 1 ch, miss 2 ch, 1 dc into next ch, 1 ch, miss 2 ch, 1 shell into next ch; rep from * to last ch, 1 tr into last ch, 2 ch, turn. 18(19–20) shells. **1st row:** [Wrong side] Work 1 shell into first shell, * 1 ch, 1 d tr into dc, 1 ch, 1 shell into next shell; rep from * to end, 1 tr into t ch, 2 ch, turn. **2nd row:** Work 1 shell into first shell, * 1 ch, 1 dc into d tr, 1 ch, 1 shell into next shell; rep from * to end, 1 tr in t ch, 2 ch, turn. These 2 rows form patt. Work 2 more rows. **5th row:** [inc row.] Work 1 d tr between first tr and shell, 1 ch, work in patt ending 1 ch, 1 d tr into t ch, 1 ch, turn. **6th row:** Work 1 dc into d tr, 1 ch, work in patt ending 1 ch, 1 dc into d tr, 2 ch, turn. **7th row:** Work 1 d tr into dc, 1 ch, work in patt ending 1 ch, 1 d tr into dc, 1 ch, turn. Rep 6th and 7th rows twice more, then 6th row once ending 3 ch, turn. **13th row:** [inc row.] Work 1 shell into 3rd ch from hook, 1 ch, 1 d tr into dc, 1 ch, work in patt ending 1 ch, 1 d tr into dc, 1 ch, 1 shell into t ch, 2 ch, turn. **14th to 20th rows:** Work in patt. Rep 5th to 20th rows twice more. 24(25–26) shells. Cont without shaping until work measures 24″(24″–25″) from beg, or required length from waist ending with a 2nd row. Cut yarn and fasten off.

BACK: Work as given for Front.

TO MAKE UP: Press each piece lightly under a damp cloth with a warm iron. Join side seams. Press seams. Sew waist length of elastic to inside of waist using casing st.

JACKET

BACK: Beg at back neck. With No. 3.50 hook make 40 ch. Work base row as given for Skirt. **Shape shoulders.** Cont in patt as given for Skirt working 14 ch at beg of next 2 rows and 14(17–17) t ch at beg of foll 2 rows. Work 18 rows without shaping ending with a 2nd row. **Shape armholes.** Inc as given for Skirt at each end of next and every alt row 4(4–5) times in all. Cont without shaping until work measures 21″(21″–21½″) from beg, or required length from back neck, ending with a 2nd row. Cut yarn and fasten off.

LEFT FRONT: Beg at shoulder. With No. 3.50 hook make 16 ch. Work Base row as given for Skirt. **Shape shoulder.** Cont in patt as given for Skirt working 14 (17–17) t ch at beg of next row. Work 4 rows without shaping. **Shape neck.** Cont. in patt working 20 t ch at beg of next row. Work 14 rows without shaping. **Shape armhole.** Inc as given for Skirt at armhole edge on next and every alt row 4(4–5) times in all. Cont without shaping until work measures same as Back from beg ending with a 2nd row. Cut yarn and fasten off.

RIGHT FRONT: With No. 3.50 hook make 16 ch. Work Base row and 1st patt row as given for Skirt. Cont in patt as given for Skirt working 14(17–17) t ch at beg of next row. Complete to match Left Front reversing shaping.

SLEEVES: Beg at top. With No. 3.50 hook make 28 ch. Work Base row as given for Skirt. Cont in patt, inc at each end of next and every alt rows as given for Skirt 8(8–9) times in all. Cont without shaping until sleeve measures 18″ from end of shaping or required underarm length, ending with a 2nd row. Cut yarn and fasten off.

TO MAKE UP: Press as given for Skirt. Join shoulder, side and sleeve seams. Set in sleeves. With right side of work facing and No. 3.50 hook beg at bottom Right Front edge and work a row of dc up right front, round neck and down left front, 1 ch, turn. **Next row:** Work 1 dc into first dc, * miss 1 dc, 2 1 ch 2 tr into next dc, miss 1 dc, 1 dc into next dc; rep from * to end. Cut yarn and fasten off. Press seams.

Mohair dress

Instructions are for a 32″/36″ bust.

MATERIALS: 19 ozs of standard mohair yarn. Crochet hook, New International size 7.00 (size K). Check your tension, as these hooks are only approximate equivalents.

MEASUREMENTS: To fit a 32″/36″ bust. 34″/38″ hips. Length to shoulder: 57″ when pressed, adjustable. Sleeve seam: 19″ when pressed, adjustable.

TENSION: 1 d tr group measures approximately 2″ at base and 1¼″ in depth.

NOTE: 1 d tr group worked by making 1 d tr, 1 ch, 1 d tr, 1 ch, 1 d tr.

BODICE AND SKIRT: Beg at neck. With No. 7.00 hook make 128 ch and join into a circle with a sl st. **1st round:** 4 ch, ★ [miss 1 ch, 1 d tr group into next ch] 3 times, miss 1 ch, 2 d tr into next ch; rep from ★ to end, ending with 1 d tr into last ch, sl st to 4th of 4 ch [16 panels each with 3 groups of 2 d tr]. **2nd round:** 4 ch, ★ 1 d tr group into centre of next 3 d tr groups, 1 d tr on each of next 2 d tr; rep from ★ to end, ending with 1 d tr on d tr, sl st to 4th of 4 ch. **3rd round:** As 2nd. **Divide for sleeves and bodice. Next round:** 4 ch, ★ [1 d tr group into centre of next 3 d tr groups, 1 d tr on each of next 2 d tr] 5 times working only 1 d tr on last rep, miss [next d tr (3 d tr groups and 2 d tr) twice, 3 d tr and 1 d tr] ★ work 1 d tr into next d tr; rep from ★ to ★, sl st to 4th of 4 ch.

This section [10 panels] forms bodice and skirt. Cont in patt until dress measures 53″ or required length, allowing 4″ for pressing. **Next round:** Work 1 dc into every st and 1 dc 3 ch 1 dc into centre d tr of each d tr group. Fasten off.

SLEEVES: Rejoin yarn to underarm into first d tr, 4 ch, ★ 1 d tr group into each of next 3 d tr groups, 1 d tr into each of next 2 d tr; rep from ★ twice more ending last rep with 1 d tr, sl st to 4th of 4 ch. [3 panels.] Cont in patt until sleeve seam is required length, allowing 3″ for pressing out. Finish as given for hem of dress. Work 2nd sleeve in same way.

NECK EDGING: With right side of work facing, rejoin yarn at centre back and work 1 dc into each ch, sl st to first dc. **Next round:** 1 ch, ★ work 2 dc tog [as follows: hook into first dc, draw through a loop, hook into 2nd dc draw through a loop, yarn over and draw through all three loops], 2 dc; rep from ★ to end, sl st to first ch. 96 sts. **Next round:** 1 ch, 1 dc into each dc, sl st to first ch. **Next round:** 1 ch, ★ work 2 dc tog as before, 1 dc; rep from ★ to end, 1 sl st into first ch. **Next round:** 1 ch, ★ 1 dc 3 ch 1 dc into next dc, dc into next dc; rep from ★ to end, sl st to first ch. Fasten off.

TO MAKE UP: Pin out to size and using a very wet cloth and a warm iron steam press. Allow to dry completely flat.

Cardigan coat

Instructions are for a 34″/36″ bust.

MATERIALS: 24 ½-oz balls standard Angora/wool blend yarn. Crochet hooks, New International sizes 4.00 and 3.50 (wool hook sizes H and G).

MEASUREMENTS: To fit a 34″/36″ bust; 36″/38″ hips. Length to centre back: 35″, adjustable. Sleeve seam: 18½″, adjustable.

TENSION: 12 sts, 1 patt, to 2½″ and approximately 7 rows to 3″ on No. 4.00 hook.

BACK: With No. 4.00 hook make 112 ch. **1st row:** 1 tr into 3rd ch from hook, ★ 1 tr into next 6 ch, 3 ch, 1 tr into next 6 ch; rep from ★ to last ch, 1 tr into last ch, 3ch, turn. **2nd row:** Miss first tr, ★ yarn over hook, insert hook into next tr and pull yarn through, insert hook into next tr and pull yarn through, yarn over hook and draw through 3 loops, yarn over hook and draw through rem 2 loops – called DT2 – 1 tr into each of next 4 tr, 1 tr 3 ch 1 tr into 3 ch loop, 1 tr into each of next 4 tr, DT2; rep from ★ to end, 1 tr in t ch 3 ch, turn. 9 complete patts plus t ch at end. This row forms patt and is rep throughout. Cont in patt, dec one st at each end of 7th and every foll 4th row until 12 sts have been dec at each end and 7 patts rem. Cont without shaping until work measures 28″ from beg, or required length to underarm. **Shape armholes.** Dec one st at each end of next 6 rows. Cont without shaping until armholes measure 6½″ from beg, omitting t ch at end of last row. **Shape shoulders. Next row:** Sl st over first 8 sts, patt to last 8 sts, turn. Rep this row twice more. Fasten off, leaving 2 patts in centre for back neck.

LEFT FRONT: With No. 4.00 hook make 64 ch. Work in patt as given for Back, dec one st at beg of 7th and every foll 4th row until 12 sts have been dec and 4 patts rem. Cont without shaping until work measures same as Back to underarm, ending at armhole edge, omitting t ch at end of last row. **Shape armhole and front edge. Next row:** Sl st over first 6 sts, patt to end. Dec one st at each end of next 6 rows, then cont to dec at front edge only on every row until 2 patts rem. Cont without shaping until armhole measures same as Back to shoulder, ending at armhole edge. **Shape shoulder. Next row:** Sl st over first 8 sts, patt to end. **Next row:** Patt to last 8 sts, turn. **Next row:** Sl st over 8 sts, fasten off. **Right Front:** Work as given for Left Front, reversing all shaping.

SLEEVES: With No. 4.00 hook make 40 ch. Work in patt as given for Back. 3 patts. Inc one at each end of 5th and every foll 3rd row, working inc into patt when possible until 12 sts have been inc at each side. 5 patts. Cont without shaping until sleeve measures 18½″ from beg, or required length to underarm, omitting t ch at end of last row. **Shape top. Next row:** Sl st over first 3 sts, patt to last 3 sts, turn. Dec one st at each end of next 6 rows. **Next row:** Sl st over first 3 sts, patt to last 3 sts, turn. Rep this row 4 times more. Fasten off, leaving 1 patt in centre.

BORDER: Join shoulder seams. With No. 3.50 hook work 1 row dc up Right Front, round neck and down Left Front, taking care that work lies flat. Turn and work 3 more rows. Fasten off.

TO MAKE UP: Press work very lightly with a warm iron over a damp cloth. Join side and sleeve seams. Set in sleeves, noting that sleeve seam should come in centre of 6 sts cast off on front armholes. Press seams.

Patchwork waistcoats

Instructions are for a 34″/36″ bust/chest. Changes for 38″/40″ size are given in brackets.

MATERIALS: 6(7) ozs standard double knitting yarn in main shade D; 3(3) ozs each of same in contrast colours A, B and C. Crochet hooks, New International sizes 4.00(4.50), or wool hooks H(I). Check your tension, as these hooks are only approximate equivalents.

MEASUREMENTS: To fit a 34″/36″(38″/40″) bust/chest. Length at back centre: 21″(24″). Underarm length: 14″(16″).

TENSION: Each motif measures approximately 3½″ × 3½″ on No. 4.00 hook; 4″ × 4″ on No. 4.50 hook.

NOTE: Quantities are based on following colour variations of A, B and C on first 3 rounds of motifs, and D is used throughout for rounds 4 and 5. Make 52 motifs in all; 9 using A, B, C and D; 9 using B, C, A and D; 9 using C, B, A and D; 9 using B, A, C and D; 8 using A, C, B and D; and 8 using C, A, B and D. Make 2 Half Motifs, 1 using D, B, C and A, and 1 using D, B, A and C.

FULL MOTIF: With No. 4.00/4.50 hook and A, make 7 ch; join into a circle with a sl st to first ch. **1st round:** With A work * 1 dc, 2 tr, 1 dc into circle, 3 ch; rep from * 3 times more, join with a sl st to first dc. **2nd round:** Break off A, join in B to first 3 ch loop, 2 ch, work 2 tr, 1 ch, 3 tr into this loop, * work 3 tr, 1 ch, 3 tr into next 3 ch loop, 2 ch; rep from * twice more, join with a sl st to 2nd of 2 ch. **3rd round:** Break off B, join in C into first 2 ch loop, 1 ch, work 1 tr, 1 dc into this loop, * 1 ch, work 1 dc, 2 tr, 1 ch, 2 tr, 1 dc into 1 ch loop between trs, 1 ch, work 1 dc 1 tr, 1 dc into 2 ch loop; rep from * twice more, 1 ch, work 1 dc, 2 tr, 1 ch, 2 tr, 1 dc into 1 ch loop between trs, 1 ch, join with a sl st to first ch. **4th round:** Break off C and join in D into 1st ch loop, 2 ch, 1 tr, * 1 ch, 2 tr into next 1 ch loop, 1 ch, work 3 dc, 1 ch, 3 dc into 1 ch loop at corner, 1 ch, 2 tr into next 1 ch loop; rep from * twice more, 1 ch, 2 tr into next 1 ch loop, 1 ch, 3 dc, 1 ch, 3 dc into 1 ch loop at corner, 1 ch, sl st into 2nd of 2 ch. **5th round:** With D work 1 ch, 1 dc into back loop of next tr, 1 dc into back loop of ch, 1 dc into back loop of each of next 2 tr, 1 dc into back loop of next ch, 1 dc into back loop of next 3 dc, 2 dc into back loop of next ch, 1 dc into back loop of next 3 dc, continue thus, working 1 dc into back of each st and inc one st at each corner as before all round. Fasten off.

HALF MOTIF: With No. 4.00/4.50 hook and D make 31 ch. **1st row:** With D work 1 dc into 3rd ch from hook, work 1 dc into each of next 12 ch, hook through next ch and pull up loop, hook through next ch and pull up loop, yarn round hook and draw through 3 loops on hook, 1 dc into each of next 14 ch, 1 ch, turn. **2nd row:** With D miss 2 dc, work 1 dc into back loop only of next 2 dc, * 1 ch, miss 1 dc, work 1 tr into back loop only of next 2 dc, 1 ch, miss 1 dc, work 1 tr into back loop only of next 2 dc, 1 ch, miss 1 dc [hook through back of loop of next dc and pull up loop] 3 times, 1 ch, miss 1 dc [hook through back loop of next dc and pull up loop] 3 times, yarn round hook and draw through 7 loops on hook; rep from * ending last rep [hook through back loop of next dc and pull up loop] 3 times, yarn round hook and draw through 4 loops on hook, 1 dc into back loop only of last dc, turn. **3rd row:** Break off D and join in B, work 1 tr 1 dc into 1 ch loop, 1 ch, 1 dc 1 tr 1 dc into 1 ch loop between trs, 1 ch, into next ch loop work 1 dc 2 tr, 1 ch, into next ch loop work 2 tr 1 dc, 1 ch, 1 dc 1 tr 1 dc into next 1 ch loop between trs, 1 ch, 1 dc 1 tr 1 dc into next 1 ch loop, 1 sl st into end loop, turn. **4th row:** Break off B and join in C, work 3 tr into first 1 ch loop, 2 ch, miss next ch loop, 3 tr 1 ch 3 tr into corner 1 ch loop, 2 ch, miss next ch loop, 3 tr into last 1 ch loop, turn. **5th row:** Break off C and join in A, work 2 tr 1 dc into first ch loop, 1 dc 2 tr 1 dc into next ch loop, 1 dc 2 tr into next ch loop, fasten off. Work 1 more Half motif in same way using colour sequence as given under Note. Sew in all ends.

TO MAKE UP: Join each motif with woven flat stitch to top loop only of last round. Join 10 motifs 4 rows deep in this way. [40 motifs.] On 5th row join 1 Half motif above first motif to form neck shaping. 1 Full motif to next motif, miss 1 motif for underarm, join 1 motif to each of next 4 motifs, miss 1 motif for underarm, join 1 Full motif to next motif and 2nd Half motif above last motif to form neck shaping. On 6th row miss Half motif and join 1 Full motif to next motif, miss underarm motif, join 1 Full motif to each of next 4 motifs, miss underarm motif, join 1 Full motif to next motif. Join top of first and last motifs of this row to 1st and 4th motifs of back for shoulders. With right side of work facing, No. 4.00(4.50) hook and D, join yarn at lower edge of right underarm and work 1 row dc all round working into back loop of each stitch only, join with a sl st and fasten off. Work round armholes in same way. Press lightly on wrong side under a dry cloth with a cool iron.

Crunchy cardigan

Instructions are for a 32" bust. Changes for 34", 36", 38", 40" and 42" sizes are given in brackets.

MATERIALS: 19(20–21–21–22–22) ozs standard 4-ply crêpe in main shade A; 1 oz in contrasts B and C. Crochet hooks, one each of New International sizes 3.50, 3.00 and 2.50 (wool hooks G, F and D). 1 buckle for optional belt, not shown.

NOTE: For International hook size check tension as this is an approximate equivalent.

MEASUREMENTS: To fit a 32"(34"–36"–38"–40"–42") bust. Length at centre back: 24¾"(25"–25¼"–25½"–25¾"–26"), adjustable. Sleeve seam: 18½", adjustable.

TENSION: 12 sts and 5 rows to 2" over patt on No. 3.50 hook.

BACK: With No. 3.00 hook and A make 110(116–122–128–134–140) ch. **Next row:** 1 dc into 2nd ch from hook and into every foll ch, 2 ch, turn. Work 3 more rows dc, turning with 2 ch. 109(115–121–127–133–139) sts, including t ch. Change to No. 3.50 hook and commence patt. **1st row:** Miss first st, * 1 d tr in next st, 1 dc in front loop only of next st; rep from * to end, 4 ch, turn. **2nd row:** * 1 dc into front loop only of d tr, 1 d tr into dc; rep from * to last st, 1 dc into front loop only of last d tr, 1 d tr into t ch, 2 ch, turn. **3rd row:** * 1 d tr into dc, 1 dc into front loop only of d tr; rep from * to last st, 1 d tr into dc, 1 dc into t ch, 4 ch, turn. The 2nd and 3rd rows form patt and are rep throughout. Work 1 row. ** Cont in patt dec one st at each end of next and ever foll 4th row until 99 (105–111–117–123–129) sts rem. Cont without shaping until work measures 18" from beg, or required length to underarm, ending with a wrong side row and omitting t ch at end of last row. **Shape armholes. Next row:** Sl st over first 6 sts patt to last 6 sts, turn. Dec, one st at each end of next 4(5–6–7–8–9) rows. 79(83–87–91–95–99) sts. Cont without shaping until armholes measure 6½"(6¾"–7"–7¼"–7½"–7¾"), ending with a wrong side row and omitting t ch at end of last row. **Shape shoulders. Next row:** Sl st over first 6(6–6–7–7–

7–8) sts, patt to last 6(6–6–7–7–7) sts, turn. Rep this row twice more. **Next row:** Sl st over first 5(6–8–6–8–6) sts, patt to last 5(6–8–6–8–6) sts, turn. Fasten off, leaving 33(35–35–37–37–39) sts for centre neck.

LEFT FRONT: With No. 3.00 hook and A make 52 (54–58–60–64–66) ch. Work as given for Back to **. 51(53–57–59–63–65) sts. Cont in patt dec one st at beg of next and every foll 4th row until 46(48–52–54–58–60) sts rem, then cont without shaping until work measures 2½" less than Back to underarm, ending at front edge. **Shape front edge.** Dec one st at beg of next and every alt row until work measures same as Back to underarm, ending at armhole edge. **Shape armhole.** Cont to dec at front edge on every alt row, sl st over first 6 sts, patt to end, then dec one st at armhole edge on next 4(5–6–7–8–9) rows. Keeping armhole edge straight, cont to dec at front edge as before until 23(24–26–27–29–30) sts rem, then cont without shaping until armhole measures same as Back to shoulder, ending at armhole edge and omitting t ch at end of last row. **Shape shoulder. 1st row:** Sl st over first 6(6–6–7–7–8) sts, patt to end. **2nd row:** Patt to last 6(6–6–7–7–8) sts, turn. **3rd row:** As 1st. 5(6–8–6–8–6) sts rem. Fasten off.

RIGHT FRONT: Work as for Left Front, reversing all shaping.

SLEEVES: With No. 3.50 hook and A make a ch of 44 (46–48–50–52–54). Beg with 1st patt row as given for Back – 43(45–47–49–51–53) sts – inc one st at each end of 3rd and every foll 3rd row until there are 73 (75–77–79–81–83) sts, cont without shaping until sleeve measures 17½" from beg, or required length to underarm less 1", ending with a wrong side row and omitting t ch at end of last row. **Shape top. Next row:** Sl st over first 6 sts, patt to last 6 sts, turn. Dec one st at each end of next 6(6–7–7–8–8) rows. 49(51–51–53–53–55) sts. **Next row:** Sl st over first 2 sts, patt to last 2 sts, turn. Rep last row twice more. **Next row:** Sl st over first 3 sts, patt to last 3 sts, turn.

Rep last row once more. **Next row:** Sl st over first 4 sts, patt to last 4 sts, turn. Rep last row once more. 9(11–11–13–13–15) sts. Fasten off. **Work sleeve edges.** With right side of sleeve facing, No. 3.00 hook and C, work one row dc round cast on edge. Cont in dc, work one more row in C, 2 rows in A and 2 rows in B. Fasten off.

BELT: With No. 3.00 hook and B make a ch 34″(36″–38″–40″–42″–44″) long, or required length. Work in dc. Work 2 rows B, 2 rows A and 2 rows B. Fasten off.

CROCHET BUTTONS: [Make 6 buttons – 2 each in A, B and C.] With No. 2.50 hook make 3 ch and join into a ring, leaving thread about 8″ long. **1st round:** Work 6 dc into circle, joining with a sl st to first dc. **2nd round:** Work 2 dc into each dc of previous round, joining with a sl st to first dc. **3rd round:** Work 1 dc into each dc, joining with a sl st to first dc. Rep 3rd round until mould is covered. **Last round:** ⋆ Miss 1 dc, 1 dc into next dc; rep from ⋆ to end, joining with a sl st to first dc. Use thread which was left at beg for sewing on buttons, first pulling it through to other side of button.

TO MAKE UP: Press work *lightly* on wrong side under a damp cloth with a warm iron. Join shoulder, side and sleeve seams. Set in sleeves. **Work Front Border.** With right side of work facing, No. 3.00 hook and A work one row dc up right front, across back neck and down left front, working 3 sts into every 2 rows. Break off A. With right side of work again facing, cont in dc and work 2 rows C and one A. Mark position of buttonholes on right front edge as follows: 1st to come ½″ from lower edge and last ½″ down from beg of front shaping, and 4 more at equal distances between. **Next row:** [Wrong side facing.] With A work in dc to 1st marked position [3ch, miss 3 dc, dc to next marked position] 5 times, 3 ch, miss 3 dc, dc to end. Work 2 rows dc in B. Fasten off. Press all seams. Sew on buttons. Sew buckle to belt.

Bikini

Instructions are for a 34″ bust. Changes for 36″ size are given in brackets.

MATERIALS: 6(7) oz balls standard 4-ply yarn. Crochet hook, New International size 2.50 (wool hook size D). 1 yd of round elastic.

NOTE: For International hook size check tension as this is an approximate equivalent.

MEASUREMENTS: To fit a 34″(36″) bust; 36″(38″) hips.

TENSION: 6 sts to 1″.

TRUNKS: ** Make 6 ch and join into a circle with a sl st. **1st round:** 2 ch, * into circle work 3 tr but keep last loop of each tr on hook, then draw a loop through all loops on hook – called 1 cluster – 5 ch; rep from * twice more. **2nd round:** * 1 dc into cluster, 3 ch, work 3 tr 3 ch 3 tr 3 ch into ch loop of previous round; rep from * twice more. **3rd round:** 1 dc into ch loop, 3 ch, * into ch loop between 3 tr groups work 3 tr 3 ch 3 tr 3 ch, into next ch loop work 1 dc 3 ch 1 dc 3 ch; rep from * twice more. **4th round:** * 1 tr into each tr, work 2 tr 3 ch 2 tr into ch loop, 1 tr into each tr, 3 ch, 1 tr into next ch loop, 1 cluster into next ch loop, 1 tr into next ch loop, 3 ch; rep from * twice more. **5th round:** * 1 tr into each tr, work 2 tr 3 ch 2 tr into ch loop, 1 tr into each tr, 3 ch, 1 dc into next ch loop, 3 ch, 1 dc into next ch loop, 3 ch; rep from * twice more. ** Rep 4th and 5th rounds twice more, then 4th round once. Work 1 dc into next tr, turn with 2 ch. **Next row:** 2 tr into ch loop, 1 tr into tr, 1 tr into cluster, 1 tr into tr, 1 tr into ch loop, 1 tr into each tr, 2 tr into ch loop, turn with 2 ch. 25 sts. **1st row:** 1 tr into each st to end, turn with 2 ch. **2nd row:** Miss first st, 1 tr into each st to end, turn with 2 ch. Rep 1st and 2nd rows 5 times more, turn with 2 ch. On **36″ size only** work 2 rows straight, turn with 2 ch. **Next row:** 1 tr into each st to last st, work 2 tr into last st, turn with 2 ch. **Next row:** 2 tr into first st, 1 tr into each st to last st, 2 tr into last st, turn with 2 ch. Rep last 2 rows 6 times more. 40 sts. Keeping waist edge straight, continue to inc 1 tr on every row at leg edge until there are 51(53) sts, ending at leg edge, turn with 26 ch. **1st row:** 1 tr into 3rd ch from hook, 1 tr into each st to end, turn with 2 ch. **2nd row:** 1 tr into each st to last 6 sts, 1 dc into next st, 1 sl st into next st, turn with 1 ch. **3rd row:** 1 sl st into each of first 4 sts, 1 dc into next st, 1 tr into each st to end, turn with 2 ch. **4th row:** 1 tr into each st to last 3 trs, turn with 2 ch. **5th row:** 1 tr into each st to end, turn with 2 ch. **6th row:** 1 tr into each st to end, turn with 9 ch. **7th row:** 1 dc into 2nd ch from hook, 1 dc into each of next 4 sts, 1 tr into each st to end, turn with 2 ch. **8th row:** 1 tr into each st to last st, 1 dc into last st, turn with 5 ch. **9th row:** 1 dc into 2nd ch from hook, 1 tr into each st to end, turn with 2 ch. **10th row:** 1 tr into each st to last 24 sts, turn with 2 ch. **11th row:** Miss first st, 1 tr into each st to end, turn with 2 ch. **12th row:** 1 tr into each st to last 2 sts, miss one st, 1 tr into last st, turn with 2 ch. Rep 11th and 12th rows 4(5) times more, then 11th row once. Turn with 2 ch. 40 sts. **Next row:** Miss first st, 1 tr into each st to last 2 sts, miss 1 st, 1 tr into last st, turn with 2 ch. **Next row:** Miss first st, 1 tr into each st to end, turn with 2 ch. Rep last 2 rows 6 times more, turn with 2 ch. On **36″ size only**. Work 2 rows straight, turn with 2 ch. **Next row:** 1 tr into each st to last st, 2 tr into last st, turn with 2 ch. **Next row:** 1 tr into each st to end, turn with 2 ch. Rep last 2 rows 5 times more. 25 sts. Cut yarn and fasten off.

TO MAKE UP: Oversew the last 25 sts to the opposite edge of the centre motif. Oversew the shaped edges of the crotch piece to the two remaining edges of the centre motif. Work a row of firm dc round leg, ending with 1 ch. Do not turn but work another row of dc right round, working from left to right instead of from right to left. Cut yarn and fasten off. Work round other leg in same way. Work a row of dc round waist, working over the elastic at the same time. Secure elastic firmly. Press lightly.

TOP: Work motif as given for Trunks from ** to **. On **34″ size only** rep 4th and 5th rounds twice more; on **36″ size only** rep 4th and 5th rounds twice more then 4th round once. **Next round:** * 1 dc into each tr, 3 dc into corner ch loop, 1 dc into each tr, 1 dc into ch loop, 1 dc into cluster, 1 dc into ch loop; rep from * twice more. Join with a sl st, work 1 ch then work another row of dc right round, but working from left to right instead of from right to left. Cut yarn and fasten off. Work another motif in same way.

TIES: Work 2 ch. Insert hook into 2nd ch from hook and draw up a loop, then draw another loop through both sts on hook. **Next row:** Insert hook into 2nd st from hook and draw up loop, then draw a loop through both sts on hook. Rep last row for 50″. Cut yarn and fasten off. Work another tie in same way.

TO MAKE UP: Sew one corner of each motif together. Press lightly. Attach a tie to each motif at top corner. Thread tie through remaining corners in opposite motifs.

Bedjacket

Instructions are for a 34″ bust. Changes for 37″, 40″ and 43″ sizes are given in brackets.

MATERIALS: 12(13–14–15) ozs of standard 3-ply crêpe. Crochet hook, New International size 3.00 (wool hook size E). 1 yd 3″ wide ribbon. 1½ yds 45″ wide chiffon for optional lining. 2 yds of swansdown for optional trimming.

MEASUREMENTS: To fit a 34″(37″–40″–43″) bust. Length to shoulder: 18½″(19″–19½″–20″), adjustable. Sleeve seam: 18½″, adjustable.

TENSION: 4 patts and 14 rows to 3″.

BACK: With No. 3.00 hook make 124(134–144–154) ch. **1st row:** 1 tr in 3rd ch from hook, 1 tr in each ch to end, 1 ch, turn. 122(132–142–152) sts. **2nd row:** 1 dc between 1st and 2nd tr, ⋆ 5 ch, miss 5 tr, 1 dc between next 2 tr; rep from ⋆ to end, 1 dc in t ch, 3 ch, turn. 147(159–171–183) sts. **3rd row:** ⋆ 5 tr in 5 ch loop, 1 ch; rep from ⋆ to end, 1 tr in t ch, 1 ch, turn. **4th row:** 1 dc in 1st 1 ch space, ⋆ 5 ch, 1 dc in next 1 ch space; rep from ⋆ to end, 1 dc in t ch, 3 ch, turn. 3rd and 4th rows form patt and are rep throughout. Cont in patt until work measures 11″ from beg, or required length to underarm, ending with a 3rd row. **Shape armholes. Next row:** Sl st over first 10(11–12–13) sts, patt to last 10(11–12–13) sts, turn. Cont in patt, dec one st at each end of next 8(10–10–12) rows. 111(117–127–133) sts. Cont without shaping until armholes measure 7½″ (8″–8½″–9″), ending with a right side row. **Shape shoulders. Next row:** Sl st over first 5(5–6–6) sts, patt to last 5(5–6–6) sts, turn. Rep this row 4 times more. **Next row:** Sl st over first 5(8–5–8) sts, patt to last 5(8–5–8) sts, fasten off.

LEFT FRONT: With No. 3.00 hook make 64(69–74–79) ch. Work in patt as given for Back until work measures same as Back to underarm, ending with a right side row. 75(81–87–93) sts. **Shape armhole. Next row:** Patt to last 10(11–12–13) sts, turn. Dec one st at armhole edge on next 8(10–10–12) rows. 57 (60–65–68) sts. Cont without shaping until armhole measures 6″(6½″–7″–7½″), ending with a right side row.

Shape neck. 1st row: Sl st over first 14(14–17–17) sts, patt to end. **2nd row:** Patt to last 3 sts, turn. **3rd row:** Sl st over first 3 sts, patt to end. **4th row:** Patt to last 2 sts, turn. **5th row:** Sl st over first 2 sts, patt to end. Dec one st at neck edge on next 3 rows, ending at armhole edge. 30(33–35–38) sts. **Shape shoulder. Next row:** Sl st over first 5(5–6–6) sts, patt to end. **Next row:** Patt to last 5(5–6–6) sts, turn. Rep last 2 rows once more, then 1st row once. Fasten off.

RIGHT FRONT: Work as given for Left Front, reversing all shaping.

SLEEVES: With No. 3.00 hook make 52(52–57–57) ch. Work first 4 rows as given for Back. 63(63–69–69) sts. Cont in patt as given for Back, inc one st at each end of next and every foll 4th row until there are 105(105–111–111) sts. Cont without shaping until sleeve measures 18½″ from beg, or required length to underarm, ending with a right side row. Mark each end of last row with coloured threads. Work further 6(6–8–8) rows without shaping. **Shape top.** Dec one st at each end of next 8(8–10–10) rows. **Next row:** Sl st over first 2 sts, patt to last 2 sts, turn. Rep this row 5(5–6–6) times more. **Next row:** Sl st over first 3 sts, patt to last 3 sts, turn. Rep this row 5 times more. **Next row:** Sl st over first 4 sts, patt to last 4 sts, turn. Rep last row once more. Fasten off.

BORDERS: Join shoulder seams. With right side of Right Front facing and No. 3.00 hook, beg at bottom, ⋆ 3 tr into end of 1st row, 1 tr into dc, 1 tr 1 ch 1 tr into end of next row, 1 tr into dc, 3 tr into end of next row, miss next dc, 1 ch; rep from ⋆ up Right Front, across Back neck and down Left Front. Turn and work 4 rows in patt as given for Back. Fasten off.

TO MAKE UP: Press work under a damp cloth with a hot iron. If lining required, cut chiffon to match crocheted pieces. Join side and sleeve seams. Set in sleeves. Make up lining and attach to Bedjacket. Sew on swansdown trimming all round fronts, neck and cuffs. Sew on ribbon to fasten front.

Instructions are for a 33″/35″ bust, when pressed.

MATERIALS: 20 ¾-oz balls of yarn. Crochet hooks, New International sizes 6.00 and 5.50. One 7″ zip fastener for back neck. For the optional lining you will need 1½ yds of 45″ wide chiffon in a matching shade.

MEASUREMENTS: to fit a 33″/35″ bust; 35″/37″ hips. Length from shoulder to hem when pressed: approximately 56″

TENSION: Approximately 4 dc to 1″ on No. 5.50 hook; it is crocheted very loosely. The circular motifs measure 3½″ in diameter when pressed.

SKIRT: Motif. 1st round: With No. 6.00 hook make 4 ch and join with a sl st to form circle. **2nd round:** Work 8 dc into circle, sl st to first dc. **3rd round:** 4 ch, 1 tr into next dc, ★ 1 ch, 1 tr into next dc; rep from ★ ending 1 ch, sl st into 3rd of 4 ch. 8 ch spaces. **4th round:** 3 ch, 3 tr into 1 ch space, ★ 1 tr into 1 tr, 3 tr into 1 ch space; rep from ★ ending sl st into 3rd of 3 ch. 31 tr. **5th round:** 9 ch, d tr into same place as sl st, ★ miss 3 tr, 3 d tr 5 ch 3 d tr into next tr, miss 3 tr, d tr 5 ch d tr into next tr; rep from ★ ending sl st into 4th st of 9 ch. **6th round:** Sl st to centre of 5 ch, 1 dc into space, 7 ch, ★★ 3 d tr 5 ch 3 d tr into 5 ch space, 7 ch. dc into 5 ch space, 7 ch; rep from ★★ ending sl st into first dc. Cut yarn and darn in end. Work 2nd motif in same way until 5th round has been completed.

6th round: Sl st to centre of 5 ch, 1 dc into space, 7 ch, 3 d tr 2 ch into 5 ch space, sl st into 3rd st of 5 ch on first motif, 2 ch 3 d tr into 5 ch space, 3 ch, sl st into 4th st of 7 ch on first motif, 3 ch, 1 dc into 5 ch space, 3 ch, sl st into 4th st of 7 ch on first motif, 3 ch, 3 d tr 2 ch into 5 ch space, sl st into 3rd st of 5 ch on first motif, 2 ch 3 d tr into same 5 ch space, 7 ch, dc into 5 ch space, 7 ch; rep from ★★ on first motif. Cut yarn and darn in end. Cont in this way until there are 8 motifs in all for the width of the skirt and 4 rows in all in depth.

SLEEVES: Work motifs as given for Skirt, having 5 motifs in all for the width of the Sleeve and 3 rows in all in depth, but leave the last row of sleeve unjoined so that although the motifs are joined at the base, the sleeve does not form a joined circle.

BODICE: 1st row: With No. 5.50 hook join yarn in sl st made by [3 d tr 2 ch sl st 2 ch 3 d tr] and make 1 dc,

Wedding dress

designed by Carmini

* 4 ch, 1 dc into 4th st of 7 ch, 4 ch, 1 dc into 4th st of next 7 ch, 4 ch, 1 dc into sl st made by [3 d tr 2 ch sl st 2 ch 3 d tr]; rep from * ending sl st into first dc. [This is now centre back edge of Bodice.] **2nd row:** 1 ch, 1 dc into same place as sl st, * 4 dc into 4 ch space, 1 dc into next dc; rep from * ending sl st into first dc. 15 dc for each motif. 120 dc. **3rd row:** 3 ch, * miss 2 dc, dc into next dc, 2 ch. Rep from * to end, sl to 1st ch. **4th row:** 1 dc, dc into each ch and dc to end. Cont in dc until underarm measures 4″ from beg, or required length measured from under bustline.

Shape armholes and divide for Front and Right and Left Back. Front Bodice. Break off yarn and rejoin on 30th st from edge. **1st row:** Work 2 dc tog, work 56 dc, work next 2 dc tog, making 58 dc in all, turn. **2nd row:** 1 ch, 1 dc into each dc to end, turn. **3rd row:** 1 ch, work 2 dc tog, dc into each dc to last 2 dc, work last 2 dc tog, turn. **4th row:** 1 ch, dc into each dc to end, turn. Rep last row 13 times more. **Shape neck. 1st row:** 1 ch, work 13 dc, turn. **2nd row:** 1 ch, work 2 dc tog, dc into each dc to end, turn. **3rd row:** 1 ch, dc into each dc to end, turn. **4th row:** 1 ch, work 2 dc tog, dc into each dc to end, turn. **5th row:** 1 ch, dc into each dc to end. Cut yarn and darn in end. With wrong side of work facing rejoin yarn to 14th dc counting from armhole edge, work 1 ch, work 13 dc, turn. **Next row:** 1 ch, work in dc to last 2 dc, work 2 dc tog, turn. **Next row:** 1 ch, dc into each dc to end, turn. **Next row:** 1 ch, work in dc to last 2 dc, work 2 dc tog, turn. **Next row:** 1 ch, dc into each dc to end. Cut yarn and darn in end. With right side of Back facing, rejoin yarn to underarm edge of Right Back. **1st row:** Work next 2 dc tog, work 28 dc, making 29 dc in all, turn. **2nd row:** 1 ch, dc into each dc to end, turn. **3rd row:** 1 ch, work 2 dc tog, dc into each dc to end, turn. **4th row:** 1 ch, dc into each dc to end, turn. Rep 4th row 16 times more, ending at armhole edge. **Shape neck. 1st row:** 1 ch, work 12 dc, turn. **2nd row:** 1 ch, work 2 dc tog, dc into each dc to end, turn. **3rd row:** 1 ch, dc into each dc to end. Cut yarn and leave end long enough to join shoulder seam. Rejoin yarn to centre edge of Left Back and work to match first side, reversing shaping. Join shoulder seam.

Complete armholes. 1st round: Join yarn to underarm edge and work 1 dc into every row around armhole, making 44 dc in all; sl st to first dc. **2nd round:** 1 ch, dc into sl st, dc into each dc to end. Cut yarn and leave long enough end to sew in sleeve. Work round other arm in same way.

COLLAR: Join yarn at centre back opening and work 1 dc into each dc all round neck. Cont in dc until collar is required depth. **Next row:** Work a row of picot all round collar by working 1 dc into 1st dc, 2 ch, then work 1 dc in same place as first dc, work 1 dc in next dc; rep to end of collar then cont working in dc only down centre back opening and up other side. Fasten off and darn in end.

TO MAKE UP: Sleeves. Rejoin yarn to sl st made by [3 d tr 2 ch sl st 2 ch 3 d tr] and work up unfinished motif side and across top as follows: **1st round:** Dc into sl st, 3 ch, 1 dc into 4th st of 7 ch, 3 ch, 1 dc into 4th st of 7 ch, 3 ch, 1 dc into 3rd st of 5 ch space, * 1 dc into 4th st of 7 ch, 1 dc into 4th st of next 7 ch, 2 dc into sl st made by [3 d tr 2 ch sl st 2 ch 3 d tr]. Rep from * 3 times more. 1 dc into 4th st of 7 ch, dc into 4th st of 7 ch, dc into 3rd st of 5 ch space. Work unjoined motif side the same as first side, dc into same place as first dc and join with a sl st. **2nd round:** 1 ch, 1 dc into same place as sl st, dc into each dc to end, join with a sl st to first dc. 44 in all. Cut yarn and darn in end. Using end left from armhole sew in sleeve. Work other sleeve top in same way. **Trim hem and cuffs.** Join yarn in sl st as given for Sleeves. 1 ch, dc into same place, work 1 dc into each of next 12 sts, work picot as given for Collar in next st, work 1 dc into each of next 12 sts, picot in next sl st; rep all way round, join with a sl st to 1 ch. Cut yarn and darn in end. **Tie Belt.** With No. 5.50 hook make a ch approximately 112″ long, or required length to tie under bust, and work 2 rows dc. Fasten off. Steam press Dress with a very wet cloth and very hot iron. Allow to dry completely flat, taking care to spread out Skirt and Sleeves without creasing. Sew in zip to back neck to come to top of collar. Thread Tie Belt through row joining Skirt to Bodice and tie at centre front. Make a lining slip if required, lightly catching shoulder seams to shoulder seams of bodice only.

Flying motif shawl

MEASUREMENTS: Length: 120″. Depth: 60″, excluding fringe.

MATERIALS: 20 ozs standard double knitting yarn in main shade A; 2 ozs of same in contrasts B, C and D; 4 ozs of same in contrast E for fringe, and 1 oz each in 6 more contrasting colours for motifs. Crochet hook, New International size 3.50 (wool hook size G).

NOTE: Dc 2 tog = work 1 dc into each of next 2 sts, leave loops of each st on hook, yarn round hook and draw through all loops on hook. [1 st dec.] Tr 2 tog = work 1 tr into each of next 2 sts, leaving last loop of each st on hook, yarn round hook and draw through all loops on hook. [1 st dec.]

MAIN SECTION: With No. 3.50 hook and A make 3 ch. **1st row:** 1 tr 1 ch 1 tr, into 3rd ch from hook, 3 ch, turn. **2nd row:** 1 tr 1 ch 1 tr, into first tr, 1 ch, 1 tr 1 ch 1 tr, into last tr, 3 ch, turn. **3rd row:** 1 tr 1 ch 1 tr into first tr, 1 ch 1 tr, into each tr to last tr, 1 ch, 1 tr 1 ch 1 tr into last tr, 3 ch, turn. Rep 3rd row until work measures 54″ from beg, or required length. Break off A. Join in B by drawing a ch through loop on hook, work 2 more ch, turn.

BORDER: 1st row: 1 tr into first tr, 1 ch 1 tr, into each tr to last tr, 1 ch, 1 tr 1 ch 1 tr 1 ch 1 tr, into last tr. Cont in patt along side edge working 1 ch 1 tr, into each row and ending 1 ch, 1 tr 1 ch 1 tr 1 ch 1 tr, into corner tr. Work along 2nd side in same way but ending 1 ch, 1 sl st into 2nd of 3 ch, 3 ch, turn. **2nd row:** 1 tr into joining sl st, 1 ch 1 tr, into each tr to first corner, 1 ch, 1 tr 1 ch 1 tr 1 ch 1 tr, into corner tr, 1 ch 1 tr, into each tr to 2nd corner, 1 ch, 1 tr 1 ch 1 tr 1 ch 1 tr, into corner tr, 1 ch 1 tr, into each tr to end, 1 ch, 1 tr into sl st, 1 ch, sl st into 2nd of 3 ch. Break off B. Join in C as for B. Turn. **3rd row:** As 2nd, 3 ch, turn. **4th row:** As 2nd. Break off C and join in D as before. **5th row:** As 2nd. 3 ch, turn. **6th row:** As 2nd. 2 ch, turn. **7th row:** 1 tr into joining sl st, 1 tr into each st to first corner, 3 tr into corner tr, 1 tr into each st to 2nd corner, 3 tr into corner tr, 1 tr into each st to end, 1 tr into sl st, sl st into 2nd of 2 ch. Break off D. Fasten off. Sew in ends. Pin out to shape and press.

FRINGE: Using 6 strands of E, 16″ long for each tassel, work a fringe along the 2 short edges, with 6 tr, between each tassel. Knot 6 strands of one tassel tog with 6 strands of next tassel, working right along fringe approximately 1″ from first knot. Trim ends.

MOTIFS: [Make 8 of each motif, using different colour for each motif.]

1st MOTIF: With No. 3.50 hook and first colour make 12 ch. **1st row:** 1 tr into 3rd ch from hook, 1 tr into each ch to end, 2 ch, turn. **2nd row:** Tr 2 tog, 1 tr into each tr to last 2 tr, tr 2 tog, 2 ch, turn. **3rd row:** As 2nd. **4th row:** As 2nd. **5th row:** 2 tr into first tr, 1 tr into each tr to last tr, 2 tr into last tr, 2 ch, turn. **6th row:** As 5th. **7th row:** As 5th. **8th row:** 1 tr into each tr to end. Fasten off. Using 2nd colour make 10 ch. Work 1st to 3rd rows of first piece, then 5th, 6th and 8th rows. Fasten off. Place smaller piece on top of larger piece. Using 2 strands of 3rd colour work 2 dc firmly round centre to hold 2 pieces tog. Cont with double yarn, making a ch of 25 sts. Fasten off, leaving ends long enough to tie to shawl.

2nd MOTIF: With No. 3.50 hook and first colour, wind yarn 10 times round forefinger and work 28 dc into ring thus formed. **1st round:** Work 1 dc into each dc to end, working into back of st only. Break off first colour and fasten off. **2nd round:** With 2nd colour work as 1st round. **3rd round:** Working into back of st only, * work 1 dc into each of next 3 dc, 2 dc into following dc; rep from * to end. Break off 2nd colour and fasten off. **4th round:** With 3rd colour and working into back of st only * work 1 dc int next dc, 2 dc, into following dc; rep from * ending 1 dc into last dc. **5th round:** With 3rd colour work as 1st round. Join in another strand of 3rd colour and with double yarn make a ch of 20 sts. Fasten off, leaving ends long enough to tie to shawl.

3rd MOTIF: With No. 3.50 hook and first colour make 5 ch and join with a sl st to form a ring. **1st round:** Work 15 dc into ring. **2nd round:** 1 dc into first dc, * 5 ch, miss 2 dc, 1 dc into next dc; rep from * ending 5 ch, miss 2 dc. **3rd round:** Into each 5 ch loop work 1 dc, 1 h tr, 5 tr, 1 h tr and 1 dc [5 petals]. Break yarn and fasten off. **4th round:** Using 2nd colour, * 1 dc round next dc of 2nd round inserting hook from back, 6 ch; rep from * to end. **5th round:** Into each 6 ch loop work 1 dc, 1 h tr, 7 tr, 1 h tr and 1 dc. Break yarn and fasten off. Using 2 strands of 3rd colour join yarn between 2 petals and make a ch of 22 sts. Fasten off, leaving ends long enough to tie to shawl.

4th MOTIF: With No. 3.50 hook and first colour * make 13 ch. 1 dc into 4th ch from hook [3 ch, 1 dc into same ch as last dc] twice, 9 ch, 1 dc into first of 13 ch [first tassel completed]; rep from * twice more but ending each tassel by working 1 dc into same ch as first tassel. Break yarn and fasten off. Join in 2nd colour into first of 13 ch with a dc and work 3 more tassels, always ending each tassel by working 1 dc into same ch as first tassel. Break yarn and fasten off. Join in 3rd colour and work 3 more tassels in same way. Join in another strand of 3rd colour and with double yarn make a ch of 24 sts. Fasten off, leaving ends long enough to tie to shawl.

5th MOTIF: With No. 3.50 hook and first colour make 16 ch. **1st row:** 1 dc into 2nd ch from hook, 1 dc into each ch to end. 1 ch turn. **2nd row:** Dc 2 tog, 1 dc into each st to end. Rep 2nd row 5 times more. Break yarn and fasten off. Using 2nd colour rep 2nd row until all sts are eliminated. Break yarn and fasten off. Join in 3rd colour and work a row of dc along all edges, working 1 dc for each st or row and 2 dc into corners. Join with a sl st to first dc. Join in another strand of 3rd colour and with double yarn make a ch of 27 sts. Fasten off, leaving ends long enough to tie to shawl.

6th MOTIF: With No. 3.50 hook and first colour make 20 ch. ★ Into 3rd ch from hook work 3 tr, but leaving last loop of each st on hook, yarn round hook, draw through all loops on hook, 3 ch, 1 dc into same ch as 3 tr; rep from ★ twice more, working into same ch as before. Break yarn and fasten off. Make 1 more flower in first colour but starting with 25 ch. Make 2 more flowers each in same way in 2nd and 3rd colours. Knot stems tog to form a bunch, leaving ends long enough to tie to shawl.

7th MOTIF: With No. 3.50 hook and first colour make 6 ch, join into a circle with a sl st. **1st round:** Work 10 dc into circle. **2nd round:** 2 ch, now work a cluster into each dc as follows: [yarn round hook, insert hook into st and draw loop through] 3 times, yarn round hook and draw through all loops on hook, 1 ch. Join with a sl st into 2nd of 2 ch, and work 15 ch. Break yarn and fasten off. Make 1 more flower in first colour and 2 flowers each in 2nd and 3rd colours. Knot stems tog to form a bunch and complete as for 6th Motif.

TO MAKE UP: Sew in ends on all motifs and press lightly. Tie motifs to shawl as required.

Giant motif shawl

Chart

Shown on the cover

1					
5	2				
3	4	3			
4	5	4	2		
2	4	3	5	1	

MATERIALS: 13 ozs of standard double knitting yarn in main shade A; 1 oz of same in contrast B; 2 ozs of same in contrast C; 7 ozs each of same in contrasts D and E; 3 ozs each of same in contrasts F and G. Crochet hook, New International size 5.50.

MEASUREMENTS: Shawl measures 70″ along long edge and 35″ at centre, excluding fringes.

TENSION: 1 square measures approximately 8″ along each side.

NOTE: 1 cl = 1 cluster made by working 3 tr but keeping last loop of each st on hook, now draw a loop through all sts on hook.

SQUARE No. 1: [Make 2.] Using 2 strands of yarn in B, make a ch of 6 sts, join with a sl st to form a circle. Cont with double yarn. **1st round:** 2 ch, 23 tr into ring. Join with a sl st to 2nd of 2 ch. **2nd round:** 4 ch, 1 tr into same ch as sl st, 1 ch, ★ miss 2 sts [1 tr, 2 ch, 1 tr] into next st, 1 ch; rep from ★ 6 times more. Join with a sl st to 2nd of 4 ch. **3rd round:** 2 ch [1 tr, 2 ch, 2 tr] into first ch sp, ★ 1 dc into 1 ch sp [2 tr, 2 ch, 2 tr] into 2 ch sp; rep from ★ 6 times more, 1 dc into last ch sp. Break yarn and fasten off. **4th round:** Join 2 strands of A into next 2 ch sp with a dc, ★ 7 ch, 1 dc into next 2 ch sp, 5 ch, 1 dc into next 2 ch sp; rep from ★ 3 times more, ending with a sl st into joining dc instead of dc. **5th round:** 2 ch, ★ 7 tr into 7 ch loop [2 ch, 1 cl, 3 ch, 1 cl, 2 ch] into 5 ch loop; rep from ★ 3 times more. Join with a sl st into 2nd of 2 ch. **6th round:** 2 ch, ★ 1 tr into each tr, 2 tr into 2 ch loop [2 ch, 1 cl, 3 ch, 1 cl, 2 ch] into 3 ch loop, 2 tr into 2 ch loop; rep from ★ 3 times more. Join with a sl st into 2nd of 2 ch. **7th round:** As 6th but ending

1 tr into each of last 2 tr. Join with a sl st to 2nd of 2 ch. Break yarn and fasten off.

SQUARE No. 2: [Make 3.] Using 2 strands of yarn in C make a ch of 6 sts, 1 tr into 6th ch from hook, 2 ch, 1 tr 2 ch, 4 times into same ch as tr, join with a sl st into 3rd of 6 ch. Cont with double yarn. **1st round**: 2 ch, 1 tr into same ch as sl st, * 4 tr into ch sp, 1 tr into tr; rep from * 4 times more, 4 tr into last ch sp. Join with a sl st to 2nd of 2 ch. **2nd round**: 2 ch, * 1 tr into each of next 2 tr, inverting hook through back of st only, 2 tr into next st, inserting hook through back of st; rep from * 9 times more. Join with a sl st into 2nd of 2 ch. Break yarn and fasten off. **3rd round**: Join 2 strands of D into first tr with a dc, * [4 ch, miss 3 sts, 1 dc into next st] twice, 4 ch, miss 1 st, 1 dc into next st; rep from * 3 times more, ending with sl st into joining dc instead of a dc. **4th round**: 2 ch, * 3 tr into ch loop, 1 tr into dc, 3 tr into next ch loop [2 ch, 1 cl, 3 ch, 1 cl, 2 ch] into next ch loop; rep from * 3 times more. Join with a sl st into 2nd of 2 ch. **5th round**: As 6th round of Square No. 1. **6th round**: As 7th round of Square No. 1. Break yarn and fasten off.

SQUARE No. 3: [Make 3.] Using 2 strands of yarn in D make a ch of 6 sts. 1 tr into 6th ch from hook, 2 ch [1 tr, 2 ch] twice into same ch as tr. Join with a sl st into 3rd of 6th ch. Cont with double yarn. **1st round**: Into each ch sp work [1 dc, 1 tr, 5 d tr, 1 tr, 1 dc], making 4 leaves. **2nd round**: * 1 dc into dc, 1 tr into tr, 2 tr into each d tr, 1 tr into tr, 1 dc into dc; rep from * 3 times more. Break yarn and fasten off. **3rd round**: Join 2 strands of A into 10th tr of 1st leaf with a dc, * 5 ch, miss 6 sts, 1 dc into next st, 7 ch, miss 6 sts, 1 dc into next st; rep from * 3 times more but ending with a sl st into joining dc instead of a dc. 8 ch loops. **4th round**: 2 ch, * 7 tr into ch loop [2 ch, 1 cl, 3 ch, 1 cl, 2 ch] into following ch loop; rep from * 3 times more. Join with a sl st into 2nd of 2 ch. **5th round**: As 6th round of Square No. 1. **6th round**: As 7th round of Square No. 1. Break yarn and fasten off.

SQUARE No. 4: [Make 4.] Using 2 strands of yarn in A make a ch of 8 sts and join with a sl st to form a ring. Cont with double yarn. **1st round**: 2 ch, into ring work [1 cl, 2 ch, 1 cl, 5 ch] 4 times. Join with a sl st into 2nd of 2 ch. **2nd round**: 2 ch, * 3 tr into 2 ch loop [2 ch, 1 cl, 3 ch, 1 cl, 2 ch] into 5 ch loop; rep from * 3 times more. Join with a sl st into 2nd of 2 ch. Break yarn and fasten off. **3rd round**: Join 2 strands of E into joining sl st with a sl st and 2 ch, * 1 tr into each tr, 2 tr into 2 ch loop [2 ch, 1 cl, 3 ch, 1 cl, 2 ch] into 3 ch loop, 2 tr into 2 ch loop; rep from * 3 times more. Join with a sl st into 2nd of 2 ch. **4th round**: 2 ch. work as 3rd round from * 4 times, ending 1 tr into each of last 2 tr. Join as before. **5th round**: As

4th round, ending 1 tr into each of last 4 tr. Join as before. Break yarn and fasten off.

SQUARE No. 5: [Make 3.] Using 2 strands of yarn in D make a ch of 4 sts and join with a sl st to form a ring. Cont with double yarn. **1st round**: Work 11 dc into ring. **2nd round**: 3 ch, * [1 tr, 1 ch] into each st to end. Join with a sl st into 2nd of 2 ch. [12 ch loops.] **3rd round**: 2 ch, 2 tr into 1st ch loop, 3 tr into each ch loop to end. Join with a sl st into 2nd of 2 ch. **4th round**: 1 dc into 1st st, * 4 ch, 1 dc into 2nd ch from hook, 1 h tr into 3rd ch, 1 tr into 4th ch, miss 2 sts, 1 dc into next st; rep from * to end. [12 points.] Break yarn and fasten off. **5th round**: Join 2 strands of F into dc of first point with a dc, * 4 ch, 1 dc into dc of next point, 4 ch, 1 dc into dc of following point, 5 ch, 1 dc into dc of next point; rep from * 3 times more, ending with a sl st into joining dc instead of a dc. **6th round**: 2 ch, * 3 tr into 4 ch loop, 1 tr into dc, 3 tr into next 4 ch loop [2 ch, 1 cl, 3 ch, 1 cl, 2 ch] into 5 ch loop; rep from * 3 times more. Join with a sl st into 2nd of 2 ch. **7th round**: As 6th round of Square No. 1. **8th round**: As 7th round of Square No. 1. Break yarn and fasten off.

THE TRIANGLES: [Make 6.] Using 2 strands of yarn in A make a ch of 6 sts and join with a sl st to form a ring. Cont with double yarn. **1st row**: 2 ch, now into ring work, 1 cl, 2 ch, 1 cl, 5 ch, 1 cl, 2 ch, 1 cl. Turn with 2 ch. **2nd row**: 1 cl into first st, 2 ch, 3 tr into 2 ch loop [2 ch, 1 cl, 3 ch, 1 cl, 2 ch] into 5 ch loop, 3 tr into 2 ch loop, 2 ch, 1 cl into last st. Turn with 2 ch. **3rd row**: * 1 cl into first st, 2 ch, 2 tr into 2 ch loop, 1 tr into each tr, 2 tr into 2 ch loop [2 ch, 1 cl, 3 ch, 1 cl, 2 ch] into 3 ch loop, 2 tr into ch loop, 1 tr into each tr, 2 tr into 2 ch loop, 2 ch, 1 cl into last st. * Break yarn, join in 2 strands of E and turn with 2 ch. **4th, 5th and 6th rows**: Work as 3rd row from * to * turning with 2 ch at end of 4th and 5th rows. Break yarn and fasten off.

TO MAKE UP: Pin out pieces to correct shape and press with warm iron and damp cloth. Using 2 strands of G and working from chart, join motifs together as follows: with right side of motifs facing each other join yarn into corner ch loop of 1st motif with 1 dc. Work 1 ch, 1 dc into corner ch loop of 2nd motif, 1 ch, * miss 1 st on 1st motif and work 1 dc into next st, 1 ch miss 1 st on 2nd motif and work 1 dc into next st, 1 ch; rep from *. Now with wrong side of work facing join 2 strands of G into one corner with a dc, * 1 ch, miss 1 st, 1 dc into next st; rep from * along all edges.

FRINGE: Using 8 strands of A 18″ long for each tassel, make a fringe along the 2 short edges, working into each alt ch loop. Now knot 8 strands of one tassel together with 8 strands of next tassel, working right along fringe approximately 1½″ from first knot. Trim ends. Pin out and press lightly.

Boleros and skirts

Instructions are for a 25″ chest. Changes for 28″, 31″, 34″, 37″ and 40″ sizes are given in brackets.

MATERIALS: 12(15–18–21–23–25) ozs standard 4-ply yarn. Crochet hook, New International size 3.50 (wool hook size G). Oddments of same yarn in contrast colours for optional embroidery.

MEASUREMENTS: Bolero. To fit a 25″(28″–31″–34″–37″–40″) bust/chest. Length: 13½″(15″–16½″–18″–18″–18″), adjustable. **Skirt.** To fit 27″(30″–33″–36″–39″–42″) hips. Length: 27″(31½″–33″–40″–40″–40″), adjustable.

TENSION: 6 tr to 1″ on No. 3.50 hook.

SKIRT

BACK: With No. 3.50 hook make 93(103–113–123–133–143) ch. **1st row:** Work 1 tr into 3rd ch from hook, 1 tr into every ch to end, 3 ch, turn. 91(101–111–121–131–141) tr. **2nd row:** Miss first tr, work 1 tr into each tr to end, 1 tr in t ch, 3 ch, turn. **3rd row:** Miss first tr, work 1 tr into each of next 4 tr, ★ 1 ch miss next tr – called sp – work 1 tr into each of next 4 tr [wool over hook, insert hook into next tr and draw loop through] 4 times into same **tr,** wool over hook and draw through all loops on hook – called B 1 – work 1 tr into each of next 4 tr; rep from ★ to last 5 sts, sp, work 1 tr into each of next 4 tr, 1 tr in t ch, 3 ch, turn. **4th row:** Miss first tr, work 1 tr into each of next 3 tr, ★ sp, work 1 tr into sp of previous row, sp, work 1 tr into each of next 7 tr; rep from ★ to last 6 sts, sp, work 1 tr into sp of previous row, sp, work 1 tr into each of next 3 tr, 1 tr into t ch, 3 ch, turn. **5th row:** Miss first tr, work 1 tr into each of next 2 tr, ★ sp, 1 tr into sp, 1 tr, 1 tr into sp, sp, work 1 tr into each of next 5 tr; rep from ★ to last 7 sts, sp, 1 tr into sp, 1 tr, 1 tr into sp, sp, work 1 tr into each of next 2 tr, 1 tr in t ch, 3 ch, turn. **6th row:** Miss first tr, work 1 tr into next tr, ★ sp, 1 tr into sp, 1 tr into each of next 3 tr, 1 tr into sp, sp, 1 tr into each of next 3 tr; rep from ★ to last 8 sts, sp, 1 tr into sp, 1 tr into each of next 3 tr, 1 tr in sp, sp, 1 tr into last tr, 1 tr into t ch, 3 ch, turn. **7th row:** Miss first tr, ★ sp, 1 tr into sp, 1 tr into each of next 5 tr, 1 tr into sp, sp, 1 tr into next tr; rep from ★ to end, 3 ch turn. **8th row:** ★ 1 tr into sp, 1 tr into each of next 3 tr, B 1, 1 tr into each of next 3 tr, 1 tr into sp, sp; rep from ★ to end but omit last sp and work 1 tr into t ch, 3 ch, turn. **9th row:** Miss first tr, ★ sp, 1 tr into each of next 7 tr, sp, 1 tr into sp; rep from ★ to end, 3 ch, turn. **10th row:** Miss first tr, ★ 1 tr into sp, sp, 1 tr into each of next 5 tr, sp, 1 tr into sp, 1 tr into tr; rep from ★ to end, ending 1 tr in t ch, 3 ch, turn. **11th row:** Miss first tr, 1 tr into next tr, ★ 1 tr into sp, sp, 1 tr into each of next 3 tr, sp, 1 tr into sp, 1 tr into each of next 3 tr; rep from ★ to last 8 sts, 1 tr into sp, sp, 1 tr into each of next 3 tr, sp, 1 tr into sp, 1 tr into last tr, 1 tr in t ch, 3 ch, turn. **12th row:** Miss first tr, 1 tr into each of next 2 tr, ★ 1 tr into sp, sp, 1 tr into tr, sp, 1 tr into sp, 1 tr into each of next 5 tr; rep from ★ to last 7 sts, 1 tr into sp, sp, 1 tr into next tr, sp, 1 tr into sp, 1 tr into each of next 2 tr, 1 tr in t ch, 3 ch, turn. **13th row:** Miss first tr, 1 tr into each of next 3 tr, ★ 1 tr into sp, sp, 1 tr into sp, 1 tr into each of next 3 tr, B 1, 1 tr into each of next 3 tr; rep from ★ to last 6 sts, 1 tr into sp, sp, 1 tr into sp, 1 tr into each of next 3 tr, 1 tr in t ch, 3 ch, turn. Rows 4 to 13 form patt and are rep throughout. Cont in patt until work measures 24″(28½″–30″–36″–36″–36″) from beg, or required length less 3″(3″–3″–4″–4″–4″), ending with a 4th or 9th row. Fasten off.

FRONT: Work as given for Back.

WAISTBAND: With No. 3.50 hook make 123(123–133–133–143–143) ch. Work 1st row as given for Skirt. Beg with 4th(4th–4th–3rd–3rd–3rd) patt row, work

Boleros and skirts

9(9–9–11–11–11) rows patt. Work 1 row tr. Fasten off.
TO MAKE UP: Press pieces on wrong side under a damp cloth with a warm iron. Join side seams, leaving 4″ open on left seam. Sew on waistband, gathering skirt to fit and allowing 1″ overlap. Fasten with hooks and eyes. Press seams. If required embroider with lazy daisy st round centre bobble, scattering round hem and waist.

BOLERO

BACK: With No. 3.50 hook make 73(83–93–103–113–123) ch. Beg with 3rd patt row work in patt as given for Skirt until work measures 8½″(9½″–10½″–11½″–11″–10½″) from beg, or required length to underarm, omitting t ch at end of last row. **Shape armholes.** Sl st over first 5(7–8–10–11–12) sts, patt to last 5(7–8–10–11–12) sts, turn. Cont without shaping until armhole measures 5″(5½″–6″–6½″–7″–7½″) from beg, omitting t ch at end of last row. **Shape shoulders. Next row:** Sl st over first 6(6–6–6–7–8) sts, patt to last 6(6–6–6–7–8) sts, turn. Rep this row 1(1–2–2–2–2) times more. **Next row:** Sl st over first 6(8–5–7–7–7) sts, patt to last 6(8–5–7–7–7) sts. Fasten off.
LEFT FRONT: With No. 3.50 hook make 43(48–53–58–63–68) ch. Work in patt as for Back, noting that on 28″, 34″ and 40″ sizes the 3rd patt row will beg as 3rd row of Skirt and end as 8th row, 4th row will beg as 9th row of Skirt and end as 4th, and so on. Cont in patt until work measures same as Back to underarm, ending with a wrong side row and omitting t ch at end of last row. **Shape armhole. Next row:** Sl st over first 10 sts, patt to end. Cont without shaping until work measures 1½″(1½″–1¾″–1¾″–2″–2″) less than Back to shoulder, ending at front edge and omitting t ch at end of last row. **Shape neck.** Sl st over first 13(16–18–21–23–25) sts, patt to end. Cont on rem 18(20–23–25–28–31) sts until work measures same as Back to shoulder, ending at armhole edge and omitting t ch at end of last row. **Shape shoulder. 1st row:** Sl st over first 6(6–6–6–7–8) sts, patt to end. **2nd row:** Patt to last 6(6–6–6–7–8) sts, turn. Rep 1st row 0(0–1–1–1–1) time more. Fasten off.
RIGHT FRONT: Work as given for Left Front, reversing all shaping and noting that on 28″, 34″ and 40″ sizes the 3rd patt row will beg as 8th row of Skirt and end as 3rd row, and so on.
TO MAKE UP: Press as given for Skirt. Join shoulder and side seams. Work 2 rows dc round all edges, working 3 dc into each st at end of front edge. Press seams. Embroider round edges as given for Skirt.

Baby's dress

Instructions are for a 20″ size. Changes for 21½″ size are given in brackets.
MATERIALS: 5(6) ozs standard 4-ply yarn. Crochet hook, New International size 2.50 (wool hook size D). 2 yds narrow ribbon. 2 small buttons.
MEASUREMENTS: To fit a 20″(21½″) chest. Length: 12½″(15″).
TENSION: One patt rep measures 1⅛″ in width.
FRONT: With No. 2.50 hook make 122(131) ch. **Next row:** 1 dc into 8th ch from hook, * 3 ch, miss 2 ch, 1 dc into next ch, 2 ch, miss 2 ch, 1 tr into next ch, 2 ch, miss 2 ch, 1 dc into next ch; rep from * 12(13) times in all, 3 ch, miss 2 ch, 1 dc into next ch, 2 ch, miss 2 ch, 1 tr into end ch, 1 ch to turn. **Commence patt. 1st row:** Miss 2 ch sp at beg of row, * [2 tr, 1 ch, 2 tr, 1 ch, 2 tr] into next 3 ch sp, 1 ch, 1 dc in tr, 1 ch; rep from * 12(13) times in all [2 tr, 1 ch, 2 tr, 1 ch, 2 tr] into next 3 ch sp, 1 dc into 3rd t ch, turn with 5 ch. **2nd row:** * 1 dc into 1 ch sp between first 2 pairs of tr, 3 ch, 1 dc into next 1 ch sp between trs, 2 ch, 1 tr into dc, 2 ch; rep from * ending with 1 tr into t ch and omitting the last 2 ch, turn with 1 ch. Rep 1st and 2nd rows 17(19) times. Fasten off. [More or less rows may be worked here if longer or shorter skirt is required.] Return to right side of foundation row. Work 76(80) dc into foundation ch, turn with 2 ch. Work 66(70) tr into dc, turn with 1 ch. ** Work 60(64) dc into tr, turn with 1 ch. Work 4 rows dc into dc. **Shape armholes. 1st row:** Sl st over 4 dc, work 52(56) dc, turn. **2nd row:** Miss 1 dc, work 1 dc into each dc until 1 dc remains, turn. **3rd row:** As 2nd.

4th row: As 2nd. 46(50) dc. Work 15(17) more rows dc. **Divide for neck. Next row:** Work 18(19) dc, turn with 1 ch. **Left Front Shoulder. Shape neck. 1st row:** Sl st into 2nd dc, work to end. **2nd row:** Work in dc until 1 dc remains, turn. Rep these 2 rows once more. **Shape shoulder. Next row:** Work 7(8) dc, sl st into next st, fasten off. With wrong side of work facing, rejoin yarn to armhole edge and work 18(19) dc, turn. **Right Front Shoulder:** Work as for Left Front Shoulder.

BACK: Work as given for Front to ** and mark centre of last row. **Right Back.** Work 30(32) dc to marker, turn with 5 ch. **Next row:** 1 dc into 3rd ch, 1 dc into each of next 2 ch for underflap, 1 dc into each dc to end. 33(35) dc. Work 4 rows dc. **Shape armhole. 1st row:** Sl st over 4 dc, work to end. **2nd row:** Work in dc until 1 dc remains, turn. **3rd row:** Miss 1 dc, work to end. **4th row:** As 2nd. 26(28) dc. Work 17(19) rows dc. **Shape neck. Next row:** Sl st over 10(11) dc, work to end. Dec 1 dc at neck edge on next 2 rows. **Shape shoulder.** Sl st over 7 dc, work to end and fasten off. **Left Back.** With right side of work facing, rejoin yarn at marker and work 33(35) dc into tr. Work 4 rows dc. Shape armhole and work to end as given for Right Back.

ARMHOLE EDGINGS: Join shoulder and side seams. With right side of work facing, sl st into seam, * work 2 tr 1 ch 2 tr 1 ch 2 tr into next dc, miss 1 dc – or row end – 1 dc into next dc – or row end – miss 2 dc – or row end; rep from * around armhole, sl st into first tr. Fasten off.

NECK EDGING: Work as given for Armhole Edging.

TO MAKE UP: Press work lightly on wrong side with a warm iron and damp cloth. Catch underflap in position. Beg at centre back and ending at centre front thread 2 lengths of ribbon through tr at waist and tie in bow at back and front. Thread ribbon through shell all round armholes and tie in a bow at shoulders. Thread ribbon through neck edging and secure ends at back. Sew on two small buttons at back opening using dc for buttonholes.

Baby's catsuit

Instructions are to fit a baby from birth to 6 months. Changes to fit a baby from 6 months to 1 year are given in brackets.

MATERIALS: 9(10) ozs standard 4-ply 100% Acrylic yarn. Crochet hook, New International size 2.50 (wool hook size D). 11 press studs.

TENSION: 1 shell of 5 tr measures 1″ in width.

NOTE: Dec worked as follows: ★ insert hook in next dc, yarn over hook and draw loop through; rep from ★ once, yarn over hook and draw through 2 loops.

LEGS: Beg at ankle. With No. 12 hook make 32(44) ch. **1st row:** 1 dc into 2nd ch from hook, ★ miss 2 ch, 5 tr in next ch, miss 2 ch, 1 dc in next ch; rep from ★ to end, 3 ch, turn. **2nd row:** 2 tr in first dc, ★ miss 2 tr, 1 dc in next tr [centre of shell], miss 2 tr, 5 tr in next dc; rep from ★ to end, ending with 3 tr in last dc, instead of 5, 1 ch, turn. **3rd row:** 1 dc into first tr, ★ 5 tr in next dc, miss 2 tr, 1 dc in next tr [centre of shell]; rep from ★ to end, 3 ch, turn. 2nd and 3rd rows form patt. Rep patt rows twice more. **Shape leg.** [inc.] 4 tr in first dc, patt to last dc, 5 tr in last dc, 3 ch, turn. **Next row:** 2 tr in first tr, miss 1 tr, 1 dc in next tr, patt to end, ending with 3 tr in last tr [i.e. t ch], 1 ch, turn. **Next row:** As 3rd patt row. Rep last 3 rows 4 times more. 10(12) shells in row. Cut yarn

60

and fasten off. Make another leg in the same way but do not fasten off. **Join legs.** Work 2nd patt row to end on leg just completed, working last shell into last dc of this leg and first dc of first leg worked, working through the 2 dcs at once. Cont in patt to end. 20(24) shells in all. Cont without shaping on these sts until work measures $16\frac{1}{2}''(17\frac{1}{2}'')$ from beginning, ending with a 2nd patt row. **Shape armholes.** Work as 3rd patt row until 3(4) shells have been worked, 1 dc into centre of next shell, 3 tr in next dc, 1 ch, turn. Cont without shaping on these sts for 8(10) more rows, ending at armhole edge. **Shape neck. 1st row:** Work in patt until 3(4) shells have been worked, turn **2nd row:** Sl st over 2 tr, 1 dc in next tr, patt to end, 1 ch, turn. **3rd row:** Work 2(3) shells, 3 tr in next dc, 1 ch, turn. **Shape shoulder. 1st row:** Work 2(3) shells, turn. **2nd row:** Sl st to centre of shell, 3 tr in next dc, ★ 1 dc in centre of shell, 3 tr in next dc. **2nd size only.** Rep from ★ once more. Cut yarn and fasten off. Return to main work. Miss 2 shells, join with a sl st into next dc, 3 ch, 2 tr in same dc, cont in patt until 8(10) complete shells have been worked, 3 tr in next dc, 1 ch turn. Cont in patt on these sts until 11(13) more rows have been worked. **Shape shoulders.** Sl st to centre of shell, 3 tr in next dc, 1 dc in centre of next shell, work 6(8) shells, 3 tr in next dc, 1 dc in centre of last shell. Cut yarn and fasten off. Return to main work. Miss 2 shells and join as for Back, and work to end. 3(4) complete shells, 3 ch, turn. Cont in patt until 8(10) more rows have been worked, ending at neck edge. **Shape neck. 1st row:** Sl st to centre of shell, patt to end, 3 ch, turn. **2nd row:** Work in patt until 2nd(3rd) complete shell has been completed, 3 ch turn. Work one row straight. **Shape shoulder.** Sl st to centre of shell, 3 tr in next dc, ★ 1 dc in centre of next shell, 3 tr in next dc [rep from ★ once more, 2nd size only], miss 2 tr, 1 tr in t ch. Cut yarn and fasten off.

SLEEVES: With No. 2.50 hook make 37 ch. **1st row:** Miss 1 ch, work 1 dc into each ch to end, 1 ch, turn. 36 dc. Work 6 more rows dc. **Next row:** [inc.] ★ 2 dc in first dc, work 5 dc; rep from ★ to end, working 1 more dc in last dc, 1 ch, turn. 43 dc. Work in patt as for Leg from 1st row, working 1 dc in first dc and missing dc, instead of ch as given in 1st row. **1st size only.** Cont without shaping in patt until sleeve measures $6\frac{1}{2}''$ from beg, or required length to under-arm, ending with a 3rd patt row. **2nd size only.** Work as given for Leg [7 rows without shaping, then 3 inc rows – 3 shells in row]. Cont without shaping until sleeve measures $6\frac{1}{2}''$ or required length to underarm, ending with a 3rd patt row. **Shape top. 1st row:** Sl st to centre of shell, patt to end, ending with 1 dc into last shell, turn. Rep last row 2(3) times more.

Cut yarn and fasten off securely.

FOOT: [Both alike] With No. 2.50 hook make 31(39) dc along foundation ch of leg, 1 ch, turn. **2nd row:** Work 20(25) dc, 1 ch, turn. **3rd row:** Work 9(11) dc, 1 ch, turn. Work 7(9) more rows on these 9(11) sts, then dec 1 st at each end of next 2 rows. 5(7) sts. Cut yarn and fasten off. Join yarn at turn of 2nd row and work 11(14) dc to end, 1 ch, turn. **Next row:** Work 11(14) dc, then 11(13) dc up row ends of foot, then 5(7) dc across toe, 11(13) dc down row ends of other side of foot, 11(14) dc to end. Work 3(4) rows without shaping. **1st dec row:** Work 20(25) dc, dec as given in Note, work 5(7) dc, dec as before, work 20(25) dc to end, 1 ch, turn. ★★ **Next row:** Dec as before, work in dc to last 2 dc, dec as before. ★★ **Next row:** Work 19(24) dc, dec as before, 3(5) dc, dec as before, 19(24) dc. Rep from ★★ to ★★ once more. **Next row:** Work 18(23) dc, dec as before, 1(3) dc, dec as before, 18(23) dc. **1st size only.** Cut yarn and fasten off. **2nd size only.** Rep last 2 rows once more, working 1 less st between decs. Cut yarn and fasten off.

COLLAR: With No. 2.50 hook make 27(31) ch. **Next row:** Miss 1 ch, work 1 dc in each ch to end, 26(30) dc, 5 ch, turn. **Next row:** Miss 1 ch, 1 dc in each of next 4 ch, 1 dc in each dc to end, 5 ch, turn. Rep last row once more, turning with 10 ch instead of 5. **Next row:** Miss 1 ch, 1 dc in each of next 9 ch, work in dc to end, 10 ch, turn. Rep last row once more, turning with 1 ch instead of 10. 52(56) dc. Work 14(15) rows dc. Cut yarn and fasten off.

TO MAKE UP: *Do not press.* Join shoulder and sleeve seams. Join foot seams up to 6th row of patt on legs. **Edging:** With right side of work facing, begin at neck edge of left front and work 70(76) dc down front to crotch, then down leg, up other side of leg, down right leg, up left leg and 70(76) dc to neck edge, 1 ch, turn. **2nd row:** Work 70(76) dc, 1 ch, turn. Work 3 more rows over this row. Cut yarn and fasten off. With wrong side of work facing, rejoin yarn with a dc to 70th(76th) dc from neck edge to Left Front and work 70(76) dc to neck edge, 1 ch, turn. Work 3 more rows dc over these 70(76) sts. Cut yarn and fasten off. With wrong side of work facing join yarn with a dc at leg seam and work in dc up leg and down to seam of left leg, 1 ch, turn. Work 1 more row dc over this row. Cut yarn and fasten off. Sew 5 press stud fasteners evenly to front borders, lapping right over left for girl and left over right for boy, placing 1 fastener at neck edge and one at lower edge. Sew three fasteners to each leg, top one near front borders and other two evenly spaced to seam. Sew on shaped edge of collar to neck edge with ends coming in centre of front borders. Sew sleeves into armholes.

Angel set

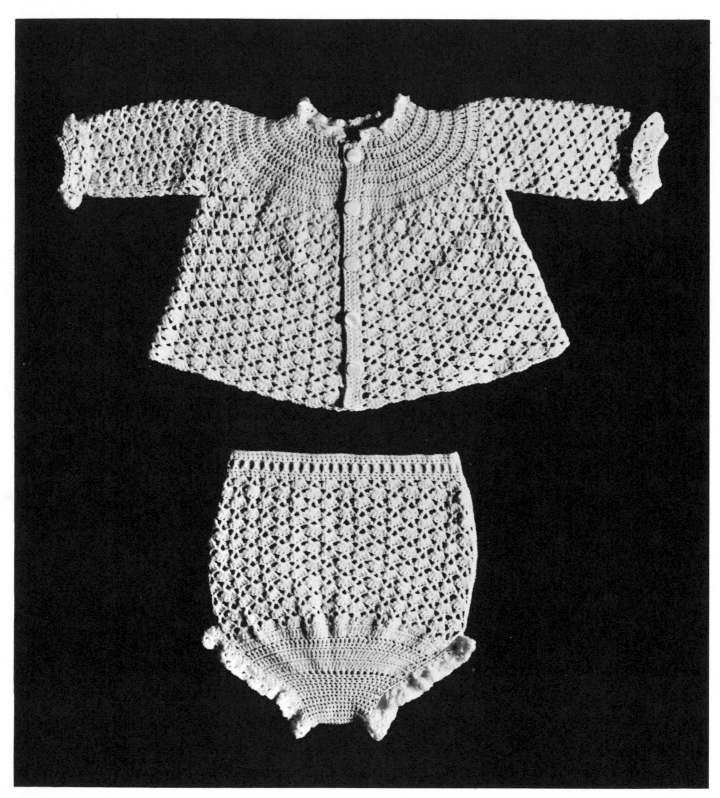

Instructions are for an 18″ chest. Changes for 20″ and 22″ sizes are given in brackets.

MATERIALS: 5(6–8) ozs standard 4-ply baby yarn. Crochet hooks, New International sizes 3.00(3.50–3.50) or wool hook sizes E(F–G). Waist length narrow elastic. 4(5–6) small buttons.

MEASUREMENTS: To fit an 18″(20″–22″) chest. Length of Top: 9″(11″–14″). Length of sleeve: 4″(6″–8″). Width of pants at widest part: 23″. Length of pants: 11″.

TENSION: 12(11–10) tr measure 2″.

NOTE: Increase by working twice into same st; decrease by taking 2 sts tog thus: insert hook into next st and pull through a loop, insert hook into foll sts and pull through another loop, wool over hook and pull through all 3 loops.

TOP: [Main part worked in one.] Beg at neck edge. With No. 3.00(3.50–3.50) hook make 61 ch. **1st row:** [Right side.] Work 1 tr into 3rd ch from hook and every foll ch to end. [59 tr] 1 ch, turn. **2nd row:** Work 1 dc in each of first 3 tr, * 2 dc in next tr, 1 dc in each of 3 foll tr; rep from * to end [73 dc], 2 ch, turn. **3rd row and every alt row:** Work 1 tr in each dc to end, 1 ch, turn. **4th row:** 1 dc in each of first 4 tr, * 2 dc in next tr, 1 dc in each of next 3 tr; rep from * to last tr, 1 dc in last tr [90 dc], 2 ch, turn. **6th row:** As 4th to last 2 tr, 1 dc in each of last 2 tr [111 dc], 2 ch, turn. **8th row:** 1 dc in each of first 5 tr, * 2 dc in next tr, 1 dc in each of next 3 tr; rep from * to last 2 tr, 1 dc in each of last 2 tr [137 dc], 2 ch, turn. **10th row:** As 8th row to last 4 tr, 1 dc in each of 4 tr [169 dc], 2 ch, turn. **12th row:** Working in dc inc in 9th tr and every foll 4th tr to last 9 sts, 1 dc in each of last 9 tr [207 dc], 5 ch, turn. **Commence lace patt.** ** Next row: 5 tr into 3rd dc, * miss 2 dc, 1 tr 2 ch 1 tr in next dc, miss 2 dc, 5 tr in next dc; rep from * to last 6 dc, miss 2 dc, 1 tr 2 ch 1 tr into next dc, miss 2 dc, 1 tr in last dc. ** [34 patt each one consisting of one 5 tr group and one tr 2 ch 1 tr sp], 5 ch, turn. **Next row:** * 5 tr in first sp, 1 tr 2 ch 1 tr into 3rd tr of 5 tr group; rep from * to end, 1 tr in top of t ch. This row forms main patt. Work 1 more row. **Divide for armholes. Next row:** Work 6 patt [consisting of 42 tr], miss next 38 tr [5 patts], beg with 5 tr in next sp, work 12 patt [84 tr], miss 38 tr, 5 tr in next sp, work remaining 5 patts, 5 ch, turn. [24 patts.] Rep patt row until 9″ (11″–14″) have been worked from neck edge. Fasten off.

SLEEVES: With wrong side of work facing, rejoin yarn to 3rd tr of 6th group in yoke, 5 ch, 5 tr in next sp, patt to last group left free, 1 tr 2 ch 1 tr in centre tr, 5 tr in hole after next group in previous row, 1 tr 2 ch, 1 tr in next hole, 1 tr in same tr as beg, where yarn is rejoined. [6 patts.] 5 ch, turn. Cont working in main patt for 3″(5″–7″), turning last row with 1 ch. **Next row:** 2 dc in each sp and 1 dc in each tr in group to end [42 dc] 1 ch, turn. **Next row:** * Working in dc work 1, dec 1; rep from * to end [28 dc] 1 ch, turn. Work 8 more rows dc. 5 ch turn. *** **Next row:** 4 tr into first dc, * miss 1 dc, 1 tr 2 ch 1 tr in next dc, miss 1 dc, 5 tr in next dc; rep from * to last 3 dc, miss 1 dc, 1 tr 2 ch 1 tr in next dc, 1 tr in last dc, 5 ch, turn. *** Work 1 more row of main patt. Fasten off. With wrong side of work facing, rejoin yarn to centre of 12th group from end and complete to match first sleeve.

BUTTON BAND: With right side of work facing, work 53(65–83) dc along Left Back edge, 1 ch, turn. Work 4 more rows dc. Fasten off.

BUTTONHOLE BAND: Work as for Button Band, making 4(5–6) buttonholes in 3rd and 4th rows as folls: Beg at neck edge work 2 dc, * 3 ch, miss 3 dc, work 8(10–10) dc; rep from * 2(3–4) times more, 3 ch, miss 3, work to end. **Next row:** Work 3 dc into each 3 ch sp.

NECK EDGING: With right side of work facing, work 48 dc along neck edge, working together every 4th and 5th tr of 1st row. Work 1 more row dc, then rep from *** to *** of Sleeve cuff. Fasten off.

PANTS: [Back and Front alike.] **Beg at top.** With No. 3.00(3.50–3.50) hook make 58 ch. Work 1 dc in 2nd ch from hook and every foll ch to end. [57 dc.] 1 ch, turn. Work 2 more rows dc, 2 ch turn. Work 1 row tr, 2 rows dc, 5 ch, turn. Rep from ** to ** of Angel Top. 9 patts. Work 15 more rows main patt. **Next row:** 2 dc in each sp and 1 dc in each tr in group to end. [63 dc], 2 ch turn. Work 1 tr in each dc to end, 1 ch, turn. **Next row:** Working in dc * work 1, dec 1; rep from * to end. [42 dc], 2 ch turn. Work 1 row tr, 1 row dc twice, then 1 more row tr turning each row as before. **Next row:** In dc dec all along row. 21 dc. Work 15 more rows dc, dec each end of 4th and 8th rows. Fasten off. Join both pieces at lower edge. With right side of work facing beg at last 2 rows of main patt and work 64 dc along each leg edge. Work 1 more row dc then rep from *** to *** as for Sleeve edge. Work 1 more row patt. Fasten off.

TO MAKE UP: Press lightly with a warm iron over a damp cloth. Join sleeve seams. Press seams. Sew on buttons. Join side seams of pants. Press seams. Thread elastic through the row of trs at top.

Matinee jacket and a Shawl

Instructions are for a 16″ chest. Changes for 18″ and 20″ sizes are given in brackets.

MATERIALS: 3(4–4) ozs of standard 3-ply nylon. Crochet hook, New International size 2.50 (wool hook size D). 1¼ yds of narrow ribbon in matching shade. 6 small buttons.

MEASUREMENTS: To fit a 16″(18″–20″) chest. Length at centre back: 7¾″(8¼″–8¾″). Sleeve seam: 5½″ (6″–6½″).

TENSION: 2 shells and 4 rows to 1″ over pattern.

BACK: Beg at left shoulder and sleeve. Make a loose ch of 48(54–60) sts. **1st row:** Work 2 h tr 1 ch 2 h tr into 3rd ch from hook – called 1 shell – * miss 2 ch, 1 shell into next ch; rep from * to end, 1 ch, turn. 16(18–20) shells. **2nd row:** Work 1 shell into each ch space in centre of shells in 1st row. ** Work 24 ch. Break off yarn. **Work right shoulder and sleeve.** Work as given for left shoulder to **, 1 ch, turn. **Next row:** Work 1 shell into each ch space as before, work 8 shells along 24 ch sts of left side and 1 shell into each ch space to end, 1 ch, turn. 40(44–48) shells. Work 12 rows in patt across all sts. Break off yarn. Rejoin yarn to 12th(13th–14th) shell from sleeve edge, work 1 shell into this space and 1 shell into next 17(19–21) shells. Work 5″(5½″–6″) on these centre 18(20–22) shells. Fasten off.

LEFT FRONT: Join yarn to neck edge of starting ch for Back. Work 1 shell into bottom centre of each shell. 16(18–20) shells. Work 7 rows in patt, ending at centre front. Work 15 ch, turn. **9th row:** Work 1 shell into 3rd ch from hook, * miss 2 ch, 1 shell into next ch; rep from * 3 times more, making 5 shells worked over ch, work in patt across rem 16(18–20) shells. 21(23–25) shells. Work 6 rows, ending at sleeve edge. Break off yarn. Rejoin yarn to 12th(13th–14th) shell from sleeve edge. Work 1 shell into this space and 9(10–11) shells to front edge. 10(11–12) shells. Work until Front measures same as Back. Fasten off.

RIGHT FRONT: Work as given for Left Front, reversing all shaping.

TO MAKE UP: Join side and sleeve seams matching patts, with a woven flat seam. **Work buttonholes and neck edging.** With right side of work facing, rejoin yarn to centre front at 7th scallop from neck edge on Right Front. **Next row:** * 3 ch, 1 sl st into centre edge of next scallop; rep from * to neck edge [6 buttonholes made], work shells round neck edge, working 1 shell into each shell and 1 sl st into each corner. Fasten off at left edge. Press lightly under a dry cloth with a warm iron. Sew on buttons and slot ribbon through sleeve edges 1 shell from edge. Slot ribbon round neck.

MEASUREMENTS: Approximately $34\frac{1}{2}'' \times 34\frac{1}{2}''$, with edging.

MATERIALS: 9 ozs of standard 3-ply baby yarn. Crochet hook, New International size 3.50 (wool hook G).

TENSION: 1 motif measures approximately $3\frac{1}{4}'' \times 3\frac{1}{4}''$.

1st MOTIF: Make 8 ch and join into a circle with a sl st into first ch. **1st round:** Work 16 dc into circle, joining with a sl st into first dc. **2nd round:** 5 ch, * miss 1 dc, 1 h tr into next st, 3 ch; rep from * 6 times more, join with a sl st into second of 5 ch. 8 spaces made. **3rd round:** Work 1 dc, 1 h tr, 3 tr, 1 h tr, 1 dc into each space, join with a sl st into first dc. 8 petals made. **4th round:** 2 ch, * 3 ch, 1 dc into top of next petal, 6 ch, 1 dc into top of next petal, 3 ch, 1 h tr into space before dc at beg of next petal, 3 ch, 1 h tr into same space as last h tr; rep from * twice more, 3 ch, 1 dc into top of next petal, 6 ch, 1 dc into top of next petal, 3 ch, 1 h tr into space before dc at beg of next petal, 3 ch, join with a sl st to first of 3 ch. **5th round:** * 4 ch, 3 tr 3 ch 3 tr into 6 ch space, 4 ch, 1 dc into h tr, 1 dc into next 3 ch space, 1 dc into top of next h tr; rep from * to end of round, join with a sl st into first of 4 ch. **6th round:** * 5 ch, 1 tr into each of next 3 tr, 5 ch, insert hook into 3rd ch from hook and work 1 dc to form picot. 2 ch, 1 tr into each of next 3 tr, 5 ch, 1 sl st into next dc, 4 ch, insert hook into 3rd ch from hook and work 1 dc to form picot, 1 ch, miss 1 dc, 1 sl st into next dc; rep from * to end of round, join with a sl st into first of 5 ch. Fasten off.

2nd MOTIF: Work as given for 1st motif until 5th round has been completed. **6th round:** 5 ch, 1 tr into each of next 3 tr, 2 ch, 1 dc into corner picot of 1st motif, 2 ch, 1 tr into each of next 3 tr of 2nd motif, 1 sl st into first of 5 ch after tr of 1st motif, 4 ch, 1 sl st into next dc of 2nd Motif, 1 ch, 1 dc into centre side picot of 1st motif, 1 ch, miss 1 dc on 2nd motif, 1 sl st into next dc, 4 ch, 1 sl st into ch before next 3 tr on 1st motif, 1 tr into each of next 3 tr on 2nd motif, 2 ch, 1 sl st into picot at end of 1st motif, 2 ch, now complete this round as given for 1st motif. Work 98 more motifs, joining one side to previous motif in same way until there are 10 motifs in a row, then join other motifs to this row in same way until there are 10 rows. 100 motifs in all.

EDGING: Join yarn to right-hand corner of 1st motif with a sl st. **1st round:** * 6 ch, 1 dc into third of 3 tr on previous round, 6 ch, 1 dc into centre picot, 6 ch, 1 dc into first of 3 tr, 6 ch, 1 dc into joining picot; rep from * all round sides, joining with a sl st to first of 6 ch. **2nd round:** * 4 ch, 1 dc into next space, 6 ch, 1 dc into next dc, 8 ch, 1 dc into next space, 12 ch, 1 dc into next space, 8 ch, 1 dc into next dc, 6 ch, 1 dc into next space, 4 ch, 1 dc into next dc; rep from * all round, joining with a sl st into first of 4 ch. **3rd round:** * 2 ch, 1 dc into next space, 2 ch, 1 sl st into next dc, 3 ch, 1 dc into next space, 3 ch, 1 sl st into next dc, into next space work [1 dc, 1 h tr, 2 tr, work 1 picot by forming 3 ch and working 1 dc into first ch, 2 tr, 1 h tr, 1 dc], 1 sl st into next dc, into next space work [1 dc, 1 h tr, 4 tr, 1 picot, 4 tr, 1 h tr, 1 dc], 1 sl st into next dc, into next space work [1 dc, 1 h tr, 2 tr, 1 picot, 2 tr, 1 h tr, 1 dc], 1 sl st into next dc, 3 ch, 1 dc into next space, 3 ch, 1 sl st into next dc, 2 ch, 1 dc into next space, 2 ch, 1 sl st into next dc; rep from * all round, join with a sl st into first of 2 ch. Fasten off.

TO MAKE UP: Sew in all ends. Press lightly under a damp cloth with a warm iron.

Crochet in the house is becoming as popular nowadays as crocheted clothes. On the following pages we give you some designs. The cushions can be adapted to make rugs or bedspreads simply by making more squares.

Double bedspread

MATERIALS: 7 lbs 13 ozs of standard double knitting yarn. Crochet hook, New International size 5.00 (wool hook J).

MEASUREMENTS: Each square measures 6″ × 6″. The flounce is 16″ deep.

TENSION: 7 tr to 2″ across.

EACH SQUARE: Make 4 ch and join into a ring with a sl st into first ch. **1st round:** 3 ch [to stand as 1 tr] 2 tr into ring [3 ch, 3 tr] into ring 3 times, 3 ch, sl st into top of 3 ch at beg of round, 5 ch, turn. **2nd round:** * 3 tr into corner sp, 3 ch, 3 tr in same corner sp, * 2 ch; rep from * to * once, 2 ch, rep from * to * once, 2 ch, rep from * to * once, 2 ch, sl st into 3rd of 5 ch at beg of round. **3rd round:** 3 ch, 2 tr in next sp [3 ch stands as first tr of this block], * 2 ch, 3 tr, 3 ch, 3 tr in corner sp, 2 ch, 3 tr in next sp; rep from * to end of round, ending with 2 ch, sl st into 3rd of 3 ch at beg of round. **4th round:** 5 ch, 3 tr in next sp, work corner sp as for previous round and continue in this manner working 3 tr in each 2 ch sp and 2 blocks of 3 tr in each corner sp with 3 ch between the blocks, ending with a sl st. Continue to work in this manner, enlarging the square on each row alternately beg rounds with 3 ch and 5 ch and continuing until 7 rounds in all have been worked. Fasten off. Work 125 more squares in same way, making 14 rows of 9 squares each.

TO MAKE UP: Lightly press each square with a warm iron over a damp cloth. Join squares neatly, 9 in a row, and press lightly again.

FLOUNCE: Each edge is worked separately. Join yarn at corner of one of the shorter edges. **1st row:** 3 ch [to stand as first tr], 2 tr in first sp, 2 ch, 3 tr in same sp, * 2 ch, 1 tr in next sp, 2 ch, 3 tr 2 ch 3 tr in next sp; rep from * to end. 3 ch, turn. **2nd row:** 3 tr 2 ch 3 tr in 2 ch sp between 2 blocks of tr, * 2 ch, 1 tr on 1 tr, 2 ch, 3 tr 2 ch 3 tr in sp between blocks of tr; rep from * to end. Rep 2nd row 4 times more, turning last row with 3 ch. **Next row:** 4 tr 2 ch 4 tr in first sp between blocks of tr, * 2 ch, 1 tr on tr, 2 ch, 4 tr 2 ch 4 tr between the 2 blocks of tr; rep from * to end. Rep last row 8 times more, turning last row with 3 ch. **Next row:** 5 tr 2 ch 5 tr between blocks of tr, * 2 ch, 1 tr on 1 tr, 2 ch, 5 tr 2 ch 5 tr between blocks of tr; rep from * to end. Rep last row 8 times more. Fasten off.

LONG FLOUNCES: Neaten other short edge with 1 row tr. Make 19 ch, miss 3 ch [3 tr 2 ch 3 tr] in next ch, 2 ch, miss 3 ch, 1 tr in next ch, 2 ch, miss 3 ch [3 tr 2 ch 3 tr] in next ch, 2 ch, miss 3 ch, 1 tr in next ch, 2 ch. Now work across one long side beg at corner of shorter flounce and noting that the extra piece just worked is sewn on over the shorter flounce. Continue as given for shorter flounce. Fasten off. Work 2nd long side to match but ending the 1st row by working across 19 ch made separately.

TO MAKE UP: Sew on the extra pieces over the short flounce at lower corners. Press out each flounce to measure 16″ in depth.

SMALL ROSETTES: Make 4 ch and join into a ring with a sl st. Into ring work 1 ch [3 tr 1 dc] 5 times, ending with a sl st into 1 ch. Fasten off, leaving a long end for sewing. Make 125 more rosettes in same way. Sew a rosette to centre of each square.

Single bedspread & Cushions

MEASUREMENTS: 8′ × 5′ without fringe.

MATERIALS: 6 lbs 12 ozs of standard double knitting yarn. Crochet hook, New International size 5.50.

TENSION: 4 tr to 1″ across.

CENTRE PIECE: Make 146 ch loosely. **1st row:** Miss 3 ch, make 1 tr in each ch to end. [144 tr including 3 ch at beg which stands as first tr.] Turn with 3 ch. **2nd row:** 1 tr in 2nd tr [3 ch at beg of rows stands as first tr throughout], 1 tr in next tr, ★ yarn over hook, hook through next tr, yarn over hook and through same tr 5 times, yarn over hook and pull through all loops on hook – called B1 – 1 tr in next 3 tr; rep from ★ to end. Turn with 3 ch. **3rd row:** 1 tr in each tr. Turn with 3 ch. **4th row:** B1 on 2nd tr from hook, ★ 1 tr in next 3 tr, B1 on next tr; rep from ★ to end. Turn with 3 ch. These 4 rows form patt. Continue in patt until work measures 8′ from beg. Fasten off.

RIGHT SIDE STRIP: Make 50 ch loosely. **1st row:** Miss 3 ch, 1 tr in each ch to end. [48 tr including 3 ch at beg.] **2nd row:** Work 4th row of patt as given for Centre Piece. **3rd row:** 1 tr in each tr. **4th row:** Work 2nd row of patt as given for Centre Piece. Cont until side strip measures same as Centre Piece. Fasten off.

LEFT SIDE STRIP: Work as given for Right Side Strip.

TO MAKE UP: Press lightly on wrong side with a warm iron over a damp cloth. Join seams. Press seams lightly.

FRINGING: Cut pieces of yarn 21″ in length. Take 4 strands of yarn, fold in half, and with right side of work facing loop these strands through the first space on one short side of bedspread, i.e. the spaces are between the tr. Rep all round bedspread, spacing strands between every 3rd and 4th tr along short sides and missing one row along long sides. **2nd round:** Take 4 strands from one tassel and 4 strands from the next tassel and knot them together 1″ down, rep all round. **3rd round:** Take the 2 ends from the original tassel and knot them together 1″ down, rep all round.

68

MATERIALS: Cushion takes 4 ozs of standard double knitting yarn in assorted colours if only one side of the cover is to be crocheted, or double this quantity if both sides are to be worked. Crochet hook, New International size 5.00 (wool hook J).

MEASUREMENTS: Cover measures approximately 16″ × 16″.

TENSION: 9 sts to 2″ over dc on No. 5.00 hook.

COVER: With No. 5.00 hook and 1st colour make 6 ch and join into a circle with a sl st. **1st round:** 3 ch, 3 tr into ring [3 ch, 4 tr into ring] 3 times, 3 ch, sl st to 3rd of 3 ch at beg of round. Break off 1st colour. **2nd round:** Join in 2nd colour to 3 ch sp, into same sp work 4 ch, 1 tr, 1 ch, 1 tr, 3 ch [1 tr, 1 ch] 3 times, into each of next 3 spaces work [1 tr, 1 ch] twice, 1 tr, 3 ch [1 tr, 1 ch] 3 times, ending with sl st into 3rd of 4 ch. Break off 2nd colour. **3rd round:** Join in 3rd colour to 1 ch sp in centre of 2 groups of tr, 1 dc in same sp, 1 ch, * 1 dc in next sp, 1 ch; rep from * to corner, 1 dc 3 ch 1 dc 1 ch into 3 ch sp at corner, rep from first * 3 times more, ** 1 dc in sp, 1 ch; rep from ** to end of round, sl st to dc. Varying colours as required rep 3rd round throughout, remembering to work 1 dc, 3 ch, 1 dc, 1 ch at each corner on every round, until work measures 16″ across. Break yarn and fasten off.

TO MAKE UP: Make another piece in same way if required or cut piece of felt 16″ × 16″ and sew to crochet piece for back.

NOTE: This cover can be made larger or smaller by adding or subtracting the number of rounds worked. If a larger cover is required remember to allow for extra yarn. A number of these squares can also be joined together to make a bedspread.

MATERIALS: 2 ozs of standard double knitting in main shade A; 3 ozs each in contrasts B, C and D. For 1 side only. Crochet hook, New International size 4.00 (wool hook H).

MEASUREMENTS: Cover measures 16″ × 16″.

TENSION: Each motif measures 4″ × 4″.

COVER: With No. 4.00 hook and B make 6 ch; join into a circle with a sl st. **1st round:** 3 ch, 3 tr into ring, * 3 ch, 4 tr into ring; rep from * twice more, 3 ch, sl st to 3rd of first 3 ch. Break off B. **2nd round:** Join in C to first 3 ch sp, 3 ch, 3 tr 3 ch 4 tr into the same sp, * [1 ch, 4 tr, 3 ch, 4 tr] into next sp. Rep from * twice more, 1 ch, sl st to 3rd of 3 ch. Break off C. **3rd round:** Join in D to first 3 ch sp, 3 ch, 3 tr 3 ch 4 tr into the same sp, * 1 ch, 4 tr into 1 ch sp, 1 ch, 4 tr 3 ch 4 tr into 3 ch sp; rep from * twice more, 1 ch, 4 tr into 1 ch sp, 1 ch, sl st to 3rd of 3 ch. Break off D. **4th round:** Join in A to first 3 ch sp, 4 ch, 1 tr 1 ch 1 tr into same sp, * 1 tr between 2nd and 3rd of 4 tr, 1 ch, 1 tr into 1 ch sp; rep from * once more, 1 ch, 1 tr between 2nd and 3rd of 4 tr, 1 ch 1 tr 3 times into 3 ch sp; rep from first * twice more [1 ch, 1 tr between 2nd and 3rd of 4 tr, 1 ch, 1 tr in 1 ch sp] twice, 1 ch, 1 tr between 2nd and 3rd of 4 tr, 1 ch, sl st to 3rd of 4 ch. Break off A. Fasten off. Sew in all ends. Make 15 more motifs in same way, changing 3 centre colours as required but keeping A for 4th round.

TO MAKE UP: With A join motifs into 4 strips of 4 using a woven flat seam and working into top loop only of last round. For Back make another square in same way and sew to first piece or cut a piece of felt to same size and sew to crochet piece. Larger or smaller covers can be made by working fewer or more squares, but remember to allow for extra yarn.

The old-fashioned beauty of delicately fine crochet

Lace table mat

MATERIALS: 1 ball Coats 3/Mercerised Crochet Cotton No. 20. Crochet hook, New International size 1.25 (cotton hook size 9).

MEASUREMENTS: Mat measures 12″ in diameter.

TENSION: First 3 rows measure 2″ in diameter.

Commence with 12 ch, join with a sl st to form a ring.

1st row: 4 ch, 29 d tr into ring, 1 sl st into 4th of 4 ch.

2nd row: 1 dc into same place as sl st, ★ 3 ch, miss 1 d tr, 1 dc into next d tr; rep from ★ ending with 3 ch, 1 sl st into first dc. [15 loops.]

3rd row: 1 sl st into first loop, 4 ch, leaving last loop of each on hook work 2 d tr into same loop, thread over and draw through all loops on hook [a 2 d tr cluster made], ★ 5 ch a 3 d tr cluster into next loop; rep from ★ ending with 5 ch, 1 sl st into first cluster.

4th row: 1 sl st into each of next 3 ch, 1 dc into same loop, ★ 6 ch, 1 dc into next loop; rep from ★ ending with 6 ch, 1 sl st into first dc.

5th row: 1 sl st into first loop, 3 ch, 5 tr into same loop, 6 tr into each loop, 1 sl st into 3rd of 3 ch.

6th row: 1 dc into same place as sl st, ★ 3 ch, miss 2 tr, 1 dc into next tr; rep from ★ ending with 3 ch, 1 sl st into first dc. [30 loops.]

7th row: 1 sl st into last loop made, 3 ch, ★ 1 tr into next loop, 3 ch, 1 tr into top of last tr [a picot made], 1 tr into same loop; rep from ★ ending with 1 tr into same loop as first sl st, a picot, 1 sl st into 3rd of 3 ch.

8th row: 6 ch, 1 tr into 4th ch from hook [another picot made], 1 tr into next tr, ★ 1 ch, 1 tr into next tr, a picot, 1 tr into next tr; rep from ★ ending with 1 ch, 1 sl st into same ch as first picot.

9th row: 1 sl st into last loop made, 6 ch, 1 tr into 4th ch from hook, 1 tr into same sp as sl st, ★ 3 ch, into next 1 ch sp work 1 tr, a picot and 1 tr; rep from ★ ending with 1 ch, 1 tr into same ch as first picot.

10th row: 6 ch, 1 tr into 4th ch from hook, 1 tr into top of tr of previous row, ★ 5 ch, miss next picot, in centre ch of next 3 ch work 1 tr a picot and 1 tr; rep from ★ ending with 2 ch, 1 tr into same ch as first picot.

11th row: As 10th, working into centre ch of 5 ch instead of 3 ch.

12th row: 6 ch, 1 tr into 4th ch from hook, 1 tr into top of tr of previous row, ★ 7 ch, miss next picot, in centre ch of next 5 ch work 1 tr a picot and 1 tr; rep from ★ ending with 3 ch, 1 d tr into same ch as first picot.

13th row: As 12th, working into d tr instead of tr and into centre ch of 7 ch instead of 5 ch.

14th row: 6 ch, 1 tr into 4th ch from hook, 1 tr into top of d tr of previous row, ★ 9 ch, miss next picot, into centre ch of next 7 ch work 1 tr a picot and 1 tr; rep from ★ ending with 4 ch, 1 d tr into same ch as first picot.

15th row: 3 ch, into top of d tr of previous row work 1 tr 2 ch and 2 tr, ★ 7 ch, into centre ch of next 9 ch work 2 tr 6 ch and 2 tr [7 ch, into centre ch of next 9 ch work 2 tr 2 ch and 2 tr] twice; rep from ★ 8 times more, 7 ch, into centre ch of next 9 ch work 2 tr 6 ch and 2 tr, 7 ch, into centre ch of next 9 ch work 2 tr 2 ch and 2 tr, 7 ch, 1 sl st into 3rd of 3 ch.

16th row: 1 sl st into next tr and into sp, 3 ch, into same sp work 1 tr 2 ch and 2 tr [a shell made over a shell], ★ 5 ch, 10 d tr into next 6 ch sp, 5 ch, into next shell work 2 tr 2 ch and 2 tr [another shell made over a shell], 7 ch, a shell over next shell; rep from ★ omitting a shell at end of last rep, 1 sl st into 3rd of 3 ch.

17th row: 1 sl st into next tr and into sp, 3 ch, into same sp work 1 tr 2 ch and 2 tr, ★ 3 ch [1 d tr into next d tr, 1 ch] 9 times, 1 d tr into next d tr, 3 ch, a shell over next shell, 5 ch, a shell over next shell; rep from ★ omitting a shell at end of last rep, 1 sl st into 3rd of 3 ch.

Complete Pineapples individually as follows:

1st row: 1 sl st into next tr and into sp, 3 ch, into same sp work 1 tr 2 ch and 2 tr, 3 ch, miss 3 ch, 1 dc into next ch sp [3 ch, 1 dc into next 1 ch sp] 8 times, 3 ch, a shell over next shell, 5 ch, turn.

2nd row: A shell over shell, 3 ch, miss 3 ch, 1 dc into next 3 ch loop [3 ch, 1 dc into next 3 ch loop] 7 times, 3 ch, a shell over next shell, 5 ch, turn. Continue this way until one 3 ch loop remains, 5 ch, turn.

Next row: A shell over shell, 4 ch, miss 3 ch, 1 dc into next 3 ch loop, 4 ch, a shell over next shell, 5 ch, turn.

Next row: [A shell over shell] twice. Fasten off. Attach thread to sp of next free shell on 17th row and complete pineapple as before. Work all in this way.

Edging. 1st row: Attach thread to 5 ch sp at base of 2 pineapples, 1 dc into same sp, 5 ch, into turning 5 ch loop at side of pineapple work 1 tr a picot and 1 tr, ★ 3 ch, into next turning 5 ch loop work 1 tr a

picot and 1 tr; rep from * twice more, 3 ch, into next shell at tip of pineapple work 1 tr a picot and 1 tr, 3 ch, into next shell work 1 tr a picot and 1 tr, ** 3 ch, in next turning 5 ch loop work 1 tr a picot and 1 tr; rep from ** 4 times more, 5 ch, 1 dc into next 5 ch sp at base of pineapple, 5 ch, into turning 5 ch loop of next pineapple work 1 tr a picot and 1 tr; rep from first * omitting 1 dc 5 ch 1 tr a picot and 1 tr at end of last rep, 1 sl st into first dc. Fasten off.

2nd row: Attach thread to first 3 ch sp between picots at side of pineapple, 6 ch, 1 tr into 4th ch from hook, 1 tr into same sp, * 5 ch, into next 3 ch sp between picots work 1 tr a picot and 1 tr; rep from * 8 times more, miss first picot on next pineapple, into next 3 ch sp between picots work 1 tr a picot and 1 tr; rep from first * omitting 1 tr a picot and 1 tr at end of last rep, 1 sl st into 3rd of 6 ch. Fasten off. Damp and pin out to measurements.

Spinning wheel and Star

MATERIALS: Coats 3/Mercerised Crochet Cotton No. 50, and crochet hook, New International size 0.75 (cotton hook size 13).

MEASUREMENTS: Motif measures 2½″ in diameter.

1st MOTIF: Commence with 10 ch and join into a circle with a sl st.

1st row: 4 ch, leaving the last loop of each on hook work 2 d tr into ring, thread over and draw through all loops on hook [a 2 d tr cluster made], * 6 ch, a 3 d tr cluster into ring; rep from * 8 times more, 6 ch, 1 sl st into first cluster.

2nd row: 1 sl st into each of first 3 ch, 1 dc into same loop, * 7 ch, into next loop work [a 3 d tr cluster, 5 ch] twice, and a 3 d tr cluster, 7 ch, 1 dc into next loop; rep from * omitting 1 dc at end of last rep, 1 sl st into first dc.

3rd row: 1 sl st into each of first 4 ch, 1 dc into same loop, * 7 ch, 1 dc into next loop; rep from * ending with 7 ch, 1 sl st into first dc.

4th row: 1 sl st into each of first 3 ch, 1 dc into next ch, * 5 ch, 1 dc into centre ch of next loop; rep from * ending with 5 ch, 1 sl st into first dc.

5th row: 1 sl st into each of first 3 ch, 3 ch, into same place as last sl st work 1 tr 2 ch and 2 tr, * 2 ch, in centre ch of next loop work 2 tr 2 ch and 2 tr; rep from * ending with 2 ch, 1 sl st into 3rd of 3 ch.

6th row: 1 sl st into next tr, 1 sl st into next sp, 3 ch, into same sp work 2 tr 3 ch and 3 tr, * 1 dc into next sp, into next sp work 3 tr 3 ch and 3 tr; rep from * ending with 1 dc into next sp, 1 sl st into 3rd of 3 ch. Fasten off.

2nd MOTIF: Work as for 1st motif for 5 rows.

6th row: 1 sl st into next tr, 1 sl st into next sp, 3 ch, 2 tr into same sp, 1 ch, 1 sl st into any sp on 1st motif, 1 ch, 3 tr into same sp on 2nd motif [1 dc into next sp, 3 tr into next sp, 1 ch, 1 sl st into next sp on 1st motif, 1 ch, 3 tr into same sp on 2nd motif] twice Complete as 1st motif.

Make 2 more motifs, joining to make a square, having 2 sps free between joinings.

FILLING: Attach thread to first free sp to left of any join on inside edge, 6 ch, * 1 d tr into next free sp, 2 ch; rep from * 6 times more, 1 sl st into 4th of 6 ch. Fasten off. This motif can be made larger if required by making more motifs and joining in same way.

MATERIALS: Coats 3/Mercerised Crochet Cotton No. 40. Crochet hook, New International size 1.00 (cotton hook size 11).

TENSION: Motif measures $2\frac{3}{4}''$.

1st MOTIF: Commence with 6 ch and join with a sl st to form a circle.

1st row: * 1 dc into circle, 5 ch; rep from * 3 times more, 1 sl st into first dc.

2nd row: 1 sl st into each of first 2 ch, 3 dc into same loop, * 5 ch, 3 dc into next loop; rep from * omitting 3 dc at end of last rep.

3rd row: 1 dc into each of next 3 dc, * 5 ch, 2 dc into next loop, 1 dc into each of next 3 dc; rep from * omitting 3 dc at end of last rep.

4th row: 1 dc into each of next 3 dc, * 5 ch, 2 dc into next loop, 1 dc into each of next 5 dc; rep from * omitting 3 dc at end of last rep.

5th row: 1 dc into each of next 3 dc, * 5 ch, 2 dc into next loop, 1 dc into each of next 7 dc; rep from * omitting 3 dc at end of last rep.

6th row: 1 dc into each of next 3 dc, * 5 ch, 1 dc into next loop, 1 dc into each of next 9 dc; rep from * omitting 3 dc at end of last rep.

7th row: 1 dc into each of next 3 dc, * 5 ch, 1 dc into next loop, 1 dc into each of next 10 dc; rep from * omitting 3 dc at end of last rep.

8th row: 1 dc into each of next 3 dc, * 8 ch, miss 1 dc, 1 dc into each of next 10 dc; rep from * omitting 3 dc at end of last rep.

9th row: 1 dc into each of next 3 dc, * 5 ch, 1 dc into next loop, 5 ch, miss 1 dc, 1 dc into each of next 9 dc; rep from * omitting 3 dc at end of last rep.

10th row: 1 dc into each of next 3 dc, * [5 ch, 1 dc into next loop] twice, 5 ch, miss 1 dc, 1 dc into each of next 8 dc; rep from * omitting 3 dc at end of last rep.

11th row: 1 dc into each of next 2 dc, * 5 ch, 1 dc in next loop, 5 ch, 4 tr into next loop, 5 ch, 1 dc into next loop, 5 ch, miss 1 dc, 1 dc into each of next 6 dc; rep from * omitting 2 dc at end of last rep.

12th row: 1 dc into next dc, * [5 ch, 1 dc into next loop] twice, 10 ch [1 dc into next loop, 5 ch] twice, miss 1 dc, 1 dc into each of next 4 dc; rep from * omitting 1 dc at end of last rep, 1 sl st into next dc.

13th row: 1 sl st into each of next 3 ch, 1 dc into same loop, * 5 ch, 1 dc into next loop, 5 ch, into next loop work 4 tr 3 ch and 4 tr [5 ch, 1 dc into next loop] twice, 2 ch, miss 1 dc, leaving the last loop of each on hook work 1 tr into each of next 2 dc, thread over and draw through all loops on hook [a 2 tr cluster made], 2 ch, 1 dc into next loop; rep from * omitting 1 dc at end of last rep, 1 sl st into first dc.

14th row: 1 sl st into each of next 3 ch, 1 dc into same loop, * 5 ch, 1 dc into next loop, 5 ch, 5 tr into next

sp [5 ch, 1 dc into next loop] twice, 10 ch, miss 2 sps, 1 dc into next loop; rep from * omitting 1 dc at end of last rep, 1 sl st into first dc.

15th row: * [4 dc into next loop, 3 ch, 1 sl st into last dc – a picot made, 3 dc into same loop] twice, 1 dc into each of next 3 tr, 7 ch, 1 sl st into last dc [a corner picot made], 1 dc into each of next 2 tr [into next loop work 4 dc a picot and 3 dc] twice, into next loop work 6 dc a picot and 5 dc; rep from * ending with 1 sl st into first dc. Fasten off.

2nd MOTIF: Work as for 1st motif for 14 rows.

15th row: [Into next loop work 4 dc a picot and 3 dc] twice, 1 dc into each of next 3 tr, 3 ch, 1 dc into any corner picot on 1st motif, 3 ch, 1 sl st into last dc on 2nd motif [a joining corner picot made], 1 dc into each of next 2 tr [4 dc into next loop, 1 ch, 1 dc into next picot on 1st motif, 1 ch, 1 sl st into last dc on 2nd motif – a joining picot made, 3 dc into same loop] twice, into next loop work 6 dc a joining picot and 5 dc [into next loop work 4 dc a joining picot and 3 dc] twice, 1 dc into each of next 3 tr, a joining corner picot, 1 dc into each of next 2 tr, complete as 1st motif.

Make required number of motifs, joining adjacent sides as 2nd motif was joined to 1st. Where 4 corners meet join 3rd and 4th corners to joining of previous 2 corners.

Lace tablecloth

MATERIALS: 10 balls Coats 3/Mercerised Crochet Cotton No. 40. Crochet hook New International size 1.00 (cotton hook size 11).

MEASUREMENTS: Cloth measures 35″ × 35″.

TENSION: Motif measures 3½″ in diameter.

1st MOTIF: Commence with 6 ch and join into a circle with a sl st.

1st row: 3 ch, 11 tr into ring, 1 sl st into 3rd of 3 ch.

2nd row: 1 dc into same place as last sl st, ★ 3 ch, 1 dc into next tr; rep from ★ 10 times more, 1 ch, 1 h tr into first dc.

3rd row: ★ 4 ch, 1 dc into next loop; rep from ★ ending with 4 ch, 1 sl st into h tr of previous row. [12 loops.]

4th row: 1 sl st into first loop, 4 ch, leaving last loop of each on hook work 2 d tr into same loop, thread over and draw through all loops on hook [a 2 d tr cluster made], ★ 5 ch, a 3 d tr cluster into next loop; rep from ★ ending with 5 ch, 1 sl st into top of first cluster.

5th row: 1 sl st into each of next 2 ch, 4 ch, a 2 d tr cluster into sp, ★ 7 ch, a 3 d tr cluster into next sp; rep from ★ ending with 7 ch, 1 sl st into top of first cluster.

6th row: 1 dc into same place as last sl st, ★ 5 ch, in next sp work a 3 d tr cluster, 5 ch and a 3 d tr cluster, 5 ch, 1 dc into top of next cluster; rep from ★ omitting 1 dc at end of last rep, 1 sl st into first dc.

7th row: 1 sl st into each of next 2 ch, 1 dc into loop, ★ 3 ch, into next 5 ch sp work 6 d tr with 1 ch between each, 3 ch, 1 dc into each of next 2 loops; rep from ★ omitting 1 dc at end of last rep, 1 sl st into first dc. **8th row:** ★ 3 dc into next sp [1 dc into next d tr, 3 ch, 1 dc into top of last dc – picot made], 5 times, 1 dc into next d tr, 3 dc into next sp; rep from ★ ending with 1 sl st into first dc. Fasten off.

2nd MOTIF: Work as for 1st motif for 7 rows.

8th row: ★ 3 dc into next sp [1 dc into next d tr, picot] twice, 1 dc into next d tr, 1 ch, 1 sl st into centre picot of corresponding point on 1st motif, 1 ch, 1 dc into top of last dc on 2nd motif [1 dc in next d tr, picot] twice, 1 dc into next d tr, 3 dc in next sp; rep from ★ once more, complete as for 1st motif.

Make 10 rows of 10 motifs, joining adjacent sides as 2nd was joined to 1st, leaving one point free on each motif between joinings.

FILLING: 1st row: Attach thread to centre picot of free point between motifs, 6 ch, 4 d tr with 2 ch between each into same picot, ★ 4 ch, miss 3 picots, leaving the last loop of each on hook work 1 tr tr into next picot, 1 tr tr into first free picot after joining of motifs, thread over and draw through all loops on hook [a joint tr tr made], 4 ch, 5 d tr with 2 ch between each into centre picot of next point; rep from ★ twice more, 4 ch, a joint tr tr over picots on each side of joining motifs, 4 ch, 1 sl st into 4th of 6 ch.

2nd row: 1 dc into same place as last sl st [2 dc in next sp, 1 dc into next d tr] twice, 8 ch, 1 dc into 3rd ch from hook, 1 dc into each of next 5 ch, 1 sl st into dc on top of d tr, ★ [2 dc into next sp, 1 dc into next d tr] twice, 4 dc into next sp, 1 dc into joint tr tr, 4 dc into next sp, 1 dc into next d tr [2 dc into next sp, 1 dc into next d tr] twice, 7 ch, remove hook, insert it into t ch of bar and draw loop through, 1 ch, miss 1 ch, 1 dc into each of next 6 ch, 1 sl st into dc on top of d tr; rep from ★ twice more [2 dc into next sp, 1 dc into next d tr] twice, 4 dc into next sp, 1 dc into joint tr tr, 4 dc into next sp, 1 sl st into first dc. Fasten off.

Fill in all spaces between motifs in same manner. Damp and pin out to measurement.

Edgings

Edging for small cloth

MEASUREMENTS: Depth of edging = 1″.
MATERIALS: 1 ball Coats 3/Mercerised Crochet Cotton No. 20. Crochet hook, New International size 1.25 (cotton hook size 9). These quantities sufficient for 2 cloths measuring $12\frac{1}{4}″ \times 16\frac{1}{4}″$.
NOTE: Before beginning cut material to required size and withdraw a thread $\frac{1}{4}″$ from edge all round. Turn back a narrow hem.
EDGING: 1st row: Attach thread to any corner, 3 dc into same place at corner, work a row of dc [14 dc to 1″] over hem and into space of drawn thread, having a multiple of 10 dc plus 7 along each side and 3 dc into same place at each corner, 1 sl st into first dc.
2nd row: 1 sl st into centre dc at corner, 4 ch, miss 4 dc, 1 d tr into next dc, ★ 5 ch, leaving last loop of each on hook work 1 d tr into same place as last d tr, miss 4 dc, 1 d tr into next dc, thread over and draw through all loops on hook [a joint d tr made]; rep from ★ to next corner, 5 ch, 1 d tr 5 ch and 1 d tr into same corner dc, 5 ch, leaving last loop of each on hook work 1 d tr into same corner dc, miss 4 dc, 1 d tr into next dc, thread over and draw through all loops on hook [a joint d tr made]; rep from first ★ omitting joint d tr at end of last rep, 1 sl st into first d tr.
3rd row: 1 sl st into each of next 2 ch, 4 ch, leaving last loop of each on hook work 1 d tr into each of next 2 ch, thread over and draw through all loops on hook [a 2 d tr cluster made], ★ 5 ch, 1 d tr into centre ch of next loop, 5 ch, miss 1 ch of next loop, a 3 d tr cluster over next 3 ch; rep from ★ to next corner, 5 ch, 1 d tr into centre ch of next loop, 5 ch, a 3 d tr cluster over first 3 ch of next loop, 5 ch, a 3 d tr cluster in same ch as last d tr and over next 2 ch, 5 ch, 1 d tr in centre ch of next loop, 5 ch, miss 1 ch of next loop, a 3 d tr cluster over next 3 ch; rep from first ★ omitting 5 ch and a 3 d tr cluster at end of last rep, 2 ch, 1 tr into first cluster.
4th row: 1 dc into loop just formed, ★ 7 ch, 1 dc into centre ch of next loop; rep from ★ to next corner, 7 ch, into centre ch of corner loop work 1 d tr 7 ch and 1 d tr; rep from first ★ ending with 7 ch, 1 dc into centre ch of next loop, 7 ch, 1 sl st into first dc.
5th row: Into each loop work 3 dc, 3 ch and 3 dc, 1 sl st into first dc. Fasten off.
Damp and pin out to measurements.

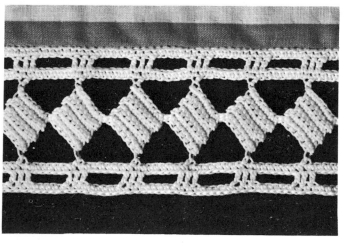

Ribbon threaded edging

MEASUREMENTS: Depth of edging: $3\frac{1}{2}$".
MATERIALS: 5 balls Coats 3/Mercerised Crochet Cotton No. 20. Crochet hook, New International size 1.25 (cotton hook size 9). To trim 1 single sheet and 1 pillowcase. 6 yds $\frac{1}{4}$" wide ribbon.
NOTE: Quad tr—quadruple treble; quin tr—quintuple treble. Quad tr worked as follows: work as for tr tr, see page 11, but working 1 more loop over hook. Quin tr worked as follows: work as for tr tr, see page 11, but working 2 more loops over hook.
EDGING: With No. 1.25 hook make ch required length, having a multiple of 12 ch plus 5.
1st row: 1 tr into 8th ch from hook, * 2 ch, miss 2 ch, 1 tr into next ch; rep from * to end, 5 ch, turn.
2nd row: Miss first tr, 1 tr into next tr, * 2 ch, 1 tr into next tr; rep from * ending with miss 2 ch, 1 tr into next ch, turn.
3rd row: 1 dc into first tr, 3 ch, miss next tr, * leaving last loop of each on hook, work 2 tr tr into next tr, thread over and draw through all loops on hook [cluster made], [4 ch, cluster into same tr] 3 times [4-cluster group made], 3 ch, miss next tr, 1 dc into next tr, 3 ch, miss next tr; rep from * omitting 3 ch at end of last rep and working last dc into 3rd of 5 ch, 8 ch, turn.
4th row: A 4-cluster group into centre loop of next 4-cluster group, 8 ch, 1 dc into next dc, 8 ch; rep from * omitting 8 ch 1 dc and 8 ch at end of last rep, 1 quin tr into last dc, turn.
5th row: 1 dc into first cluster, * [4 dc into next loop, 1 dc into next cluster] 3 times, 1 dc into next cluster; rep from * omitting 1 dc at end of last rep, 1 ch, turn.
6th row: Lifting front half of st only work 1 dc into each dc, 8 ch, turn.
7th row: Miss first 6 dc, * [1 cluster into next dc, 4 ch] 3 times, 1 cl into next dc, 8 ch, miss 5 dc, 1 dc into each of next 2 dc, 8 ch, miss 5 dc; rep from * omitting 8 ch 2 dc and 8 ch at end of last rep, 1 quin tr into last dc, turn.
8th row: 1 dc into first cluster, * 6 ch, a 4-cluster group into centre loop of next 4 tr group, 6 ch, 1 dc into last cluster of same group, 1 dc into first cluster of next group; rep from * omitting 6 ch and 2 dc at end of last rep, 1 quad tr into last cluster of group, turn.

9th row: * [1 dc into next cluster, 4 dc into next loop] 3 times, 1 dc into next cluster; rep from * to end, 1 ch, turn.
10th row: As 6th row, turning with 1 ch instead of 8 ch.
11th row: Lifting back half of st only work 1 dc into each dc. Fasten off.
HEADING: Attach thread to first of foundation ch, 3 ch.
1st row: Rep from * to * of 3rd row of Edging, working clusters into base of tr on foundation ch and omitting 3 ch 1 dc and 3 ch at end of last rep, 1 tr into 3rd of 5 ch, turn.
2nd row: As 5th row of Edging.
3rd row: As 11th row of Edging. Fasten off.
Damp and pin out to measurements. Weave ribbon through first 2 rows of edging, sew in ends. Sew foundation ch to edge of material being trimmed.

Edging for mats

MEASUREMENTS: Depth of edging: $1\frac{1}{2}$".
MATERIALS: 2 balls Coats 3/Mercerised Crochet Cotton No. 20. Crochet hook, New International size 1.25 (cotton hook size 9). These quantities are sufficient for 4 place mats 11" × 16".
DIAMOND EDGE: With No. 1.25 hook make 8 ch.
1st row: 1 dc into 2nd ch from hook, 1 dc into each ch, 1 ch, turn.
2nd to 5th rows: Working only into back half of each st, work 1 dc into each dc, 1 ch, turn.
6th row: As 2nd row, ending with 8 ch, turn. [Diamond made.] Rep 1st to 6th row 17 times more, or required length, omitting turning ch at end of last rep, 9 ch, do not turn.
SIDE EDGE: **1st row:** 1 dc into free point of last diamond worked, * 7 ch, 1 dc into free point of next diamond; rep from * ending with 5 ch, 1 d tr into first of foundation ch, 1 ch, turn.
2nd row: [Right side.] 1 dc into first d tr, 1 dc into each of next 5 ch, * 1 dc into next dc, 1 dc into each of next 7 ch; rep from * ending with 1 dc into next dc, 1 dc into each of next 6 ch, 3 ch, turn.
3rd row: Miss first dc, 1 tr into next dc, 3 ch, miss 3 dc, * 1 tr into each of next 3 dc, 5 ch, miss 5 dc; rep from * ending with 1 tr into each of next 3 dc, 3 ch, miss 3 dc, 1 tr into each of next 2 dc, 1 ch, turn.
4th row: 1 dc into each st. Fasten off. With wrong side facing, attach thread to first of foundation ch, 9 ch, and work along opposite side to correspond. Make 3 more edgings in same way.
Damp and pin out to measurements.
Sew crochet edgings across short ends of mats or as required.

Trimmings

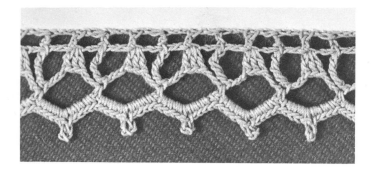

Picot lace trimming

MEASUREMENTS: 1″ in depth.
MATERIALS: Coats 3/Mercerised Crochet Cotton No. 20. **Foundation row:** With crochet hook, New International size 1.25 (cotton hook size 9) make 8 ch. 1 tr into 8th ch from hook, * 5 ch, turn, miss 2 ch, 1 tr into next ch; rep from * for length required, having a multiple of 2 spaces, 8 ch, turn and continue along side.

1st row: 3 tr into same place as last tr, * 3 ch, 1 tr tr into top of next tr, 3 ch, 3 tr into base of same tr; rep from * ending with 3 ch, miss 2 ch, 1 tr tr into next ch, 1 ch, turn.

2nd row: 1 dc into first tr tr, * 7 ch, 1 dc into next tr tr; rep from * ending with 7 ch, 1 dc into 5th of 8 ch, 1 ch, turn.

3rd row: Into each loop work 5 dc 4 ch, 1 sl st into 4th ch from hook [picot made] and 5 dc, 1 sl st into first dc of previous row. Fasten off.

Damp and pin out to measurements.

Trimming for cloth and napkins

MEASUREMENTS: Depth of edging: 1″.
MATERIALS: 4 balls Coats 3/Mercerised Crochet Cotton No. 20. Crochet hook, New International size 1.25 (cotton hook size 9). This is sufficient for a cloth 36″ square and 3 napkins 12″ square.

MAIN SECTION: With No. 1.25 hook make * 4 ch, leaving last loop of each on hook work 2 d tr into 4th ch from hook, thread over and draw through all loops on hook [a 2 d tr cl made]; rep from * for length required to go round cloth having 2 cls extra for each, corner and taking care to have the same number of cls for opposite side, 1 sl st into base of first cl, do not fasten off.

HEADING: 1st row: [right side] 3 ch, a 2 d tr cl into same place as sl st, miss base of next cl, a 3 d tr cl into base of next cl [corner made], * 3 ch, a 3 d tr cl into base of next cl; rep from * for measurement required to next corner, miss base of next cl, a 3 d tr cl into base of next cl [another corner made] complete other sides and corners to correspond, ending with 1 sl st into first cl.

2nd row: 5 dc into each sp, 1 sl st into first dc. Fasten off.

EDGING: 1st row: With right side facing attach thread to join of Main Section, 3 ch, a 2 d tr cl into same place as join, * 3 ch, a 3 d tr cl into base of next cl of Heading; rep from * along side, 3 ch, into base of next cl of Main Section work a 3 d tr cl, 3 ch and a 3 d tr cl [corner made], 3 ch, complete other sides and corners to correspond, ending with 1 sl st into first cl.

2nd row: Into each sp work 3 dc, 3 ch, 1 sl st into last dc and 2 dc, 1 sl st into first dc. Fasten off.

Damp and pin out to measurements. Sew edgings round cloth and napkins.

Pointed-lace trimming

MEASUREMENTS: Approximately 2¼″ in depth.
MATERIALS: Coats 3/Mercerised Crochet Cotton No. 20

1st row: With crochet hook, New International size 1.25 (cotton hook size 9) make 6 ch, 1 quad tr into 6th ch from hook, * 6 ch, 1 quad tr into last quad tr; rep from * for length required.

2nd row: * Into next loop work 5 dc 4 ch 5 dc; rep from * to end of row, 1 sl st into base of first quad tr, now working along other side of 1st row, into each loop work 5 dc 4 ch 5 dc, 1 sl st into last quad tr.

3rd row: 6 ch, 1 d tr into first 4 ch loop, * into same loop work 2 d tr 6 ch [1 tr into last d tr] and 2 d tr, leaving last loop of each on hook work 1 d tr into same loop as last d tr and 1 d tr into next loop, thread over and draw through all loops on hook; rep from * to end of row, into same loop as last d tr work 2 d tr 6 ch [1 tr into last d tr] and 3 d tr, 6 ch, 1 sl st into next sl st [at end of row], ** 6 ch, now working along other side, 1 d tr into first loop; rep from * to **.

4th row: 7 dc into first loop, 1 dc into each of next 3 d tr, * into next loop work 4 dc 4 ch [1 sl st into last dc] and 3 dc, ** 1 dc into each of next 2 d tr, miss next st, 1 dc into each of next 2 d tr; rep from * to end of row, ending last rep at **, 1 dc into each of next 3 d tr, 7 dc into each of next 2 loops, 1 dc into each of next 3 d tr; rep from * to end of row, ending last rep at **, 1 dc into each of next 3 d tr, 7 dc into next loop, 1 sl st into first dc. Fasten off.
Damp and pin out to measurements.

Shell trimming

MEASUREMENTS: 1¼″ in depth.
MATERIALS: Coats 3/Mercerised Crochet Cotton No. 20.

1st row: With crochet hook, New International size 1.25 (cotton hook size 9) make 10 ch.

2nd row: 1 tr into 7th ch from hook, 2 tr into each of next 3 ch, 4 ch, turn.

3rd row: Miss first 2 tr, 1 tr into next tr [1 ch, miss next tr, 1 tr into next tr] twice, 3 ch, 7 tr into next loop, 4 ch, turn.
Rep 3rd row for length required, omitting 6 tr and 4 ch turn at end of last rep.

Heading: 2 dc over bar of last tr worked, * 5 ch, 3 tr into next turning sp; rep from * ending with 4 ch, 1 d tr into foundation loop. Fasten off.

Edging: Attach thread to last sp worked on opposite side 3 ch, into same sp work 1 tr 2 ch 2 tr, * 4 ch, 1 dc into 3rd ch from hook, 1 ch, into next turning sp work 2 tr 2 ch and 2 tr; rep from * to end. Fasten off.
Damp and pin out to measurements.

Braids

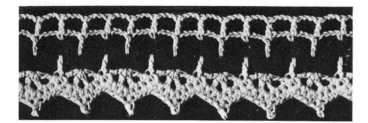

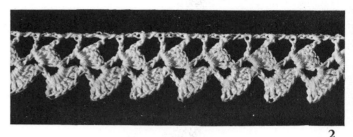

1

2

No. 1
MATERIALS: Coats 3/Mercerised Crochet Cotton No. 20. New International crochet hook size **1.25** (cotton hook size 9).

TENSION: Width of braid: 1⅛".

1st row: Take a piece of braid of required length. Attach thread to first peak, 1 dc into same place as join, * 3 ch, 1 tr into centre of curve, 3 ch, 1 dc into next peak; rep from * to end, 6 ch, turn.

2nd row: * 1 tr into next tr, 3 ch, 1 tr into next dc, 3 ch; rep from * omitting 3 ch at end. Fasten off.

EDGING: 1st row: With right side facing, attach thread to centre of first curve on opposite side of braid, 3 ch, * into next peak work [1 tr, 2ch] 3 times and 1 tr, 1 tr into centre of next curve; rep from * ending with 1 ch, turn.

2nd row: 1 dc into first tr, * 2 dc into next sp, 3 dc into next sp, 2 dc into next sp, miss 1 tr, 1 dc into next tr; rep from * working last dc into 3rd of 3 ch, 1 ch, turn.

3rd row: 1 dc into each of next 5 dc, * 3 ch, 1 dc into last dc – a picot made – 1 dc into each of next 8 dc; rep from * omitting 4 dc at end of last rep. Fasten off.

No. 2
MATERIALS: Coats 3/Mercerised Crochet Cotton No. 20. Crochet hook, New International size **1.25** (cotton hook size 9).

TENSION: Width of braid: ¾".

7 ch, 6 tr into 4th ch from hook, 2 ch, 1 tr into same ch, 2 ch, miss 2 ch, 1 tr into next ch, 6 ch, turn, * miss 1 sp, into next sp work 4 tr 2 ch and 1 tr, 3 ch, turn, into next sp work 6 tr 2 ch and 1 tr 2 ch, 1 tr into 3rd of 6 ch, 6 ch, turn; rep from * for length required. Fasten off.

No. 3
MATERIALS: Coats 3/Mercerised Crochet Cotton No. 20. Crochet hook, New International size **1.25** (cotton hook size 9).

TENSION: Width of braid: ⅝".

Start with a chain, a multiple of 10 ch plus 2.

1st row: 1 dc into 2nd ch from hook, * 5 ch, miss 4 ch 1 dc into next ch; rep from * ending with 5 ch, turn.

2nd row: 1 dc into first loop, * 6 ch, 1 dc into next loop; rep from * ending with 2 ch, 1 tr into next dc, 1 ch, turn.

3rd row: 1 dc into first tr, * 2 ch, into next loop work [2 tr, 3 ch] twice and 2 tr, 2 ch, 1 dc into next loop; rep from * working last dc into 3rd of 5 ch. Fasten off.

No. 4
MATERIALS: Coats 3/Mercerised Crochet Cotton No. 20. Crochet hook, New International size **1.25** (cotton hook size 9).

TENSION: Width of braid: ⅝".

Commence with a length of ch having a multiple of 8 ch plus 2.

1st row: 1 dc into 2nd ch from hook, 1 dc into next ch, * 3 ch, miss 2 ch, 1 tr into next ch, 3 ch, miss 2 ch, 1 dc into each of next 3 ch; rep from * omitting 1 dc at end of last rep, 6 ch, turn.

2nd row: * 1 dc into next loop, 1 dc into next tr, 1 dc into next loop, 3 ch, miss 1 dc, 1 tr into next dc, 3 ch; rep from * omitting 3 ch at end of last rep, 1 ch, turn.

3rd row: 1 dc into first tr, * 1 dc into next loop, 3 ch, miss 1 dc, 1 tr into next dc, 4 ch, 1 dc into last tr, 3 ch, 1 dc into next loop, 1 dc into next tr; rep from * working last dc into 3rd of 6 ch. Fasten off.

3

4